# Veiled GLORY

## Women Reflecting the Image of God

To Carolyn,
The Lord delights
in you.
Isaiah 62:3,4
Elaine V. Yoder

Elaine V. Yoder

International Standard Book Number: 978-1-7359070-4-8

Cover designed by Diane Horst, Light by Reflection.

Printed by:

LITTLE MOUNTAIN PRINTING

Myerstown, PA • littlemountainprinting.com

# Dedication

*To all women who seek to express the Creator's exquisite feminine image and design in their lives*

*Isaiah 62:1-5*

# Acknowledgements

Dr. Donna Wallace – your skillful guidance of the dissertation and this project, your support and belief in the concepts and need of this material, offered me the impetus I needed to press on these many years.

Little Mountain Printing – for graphic and editorial skills to produce this beautiful document.

Light by Reflection, Diane Horst – for skillfully developing beautiful images to enhance the message of the manuscript.

Frieda Graber – friendship and conversation, writing retreat space for focused time to write.

Janessa Miller and Brenda Hershberger – for the final editorial push to the finish line.

Above all, our Creator God, for the creative image in which we have been made, that reveals the desire of Your heart to be known by Your people.

*Elaine*

# Endorsements

The beauty and gift of being feminine is often lost, sometimes because of abuse, male dominance, or gender confusion. Elaine invites the reader to see a bigger perspective – that God has purpose and design in creating the differences of male and female as valuable counterparts. Each gender portrays a part of God's character, which together gives us a more complete picture of God. If we as women embrace that framework, it will add dimension to our daily tasks and roles.

*– Frieda Graber, mother, grandmother,*
*Counselor at Connections Counseling Services*

"Veiled Glory" takes us on a journey revealing the value, beauty, and mystery of our femininity. Through Bible narrative and personal experience, Elaine winds her way through a maze leaving me with the thrill of being a woman made in the image of God, valued and important in the scheme of life.

*Cathie Gingerich, wife, mother, counselor*

"Veiled Glory" brings refreshing clarity to the ways women distinctly and gloriously radiate the image of God. Using the stories of women throughout scripture, the author draws particular attention to the ways Christ affirmed the dignity, calling, and personhood of women around Him.

*Randall Martin, husband, father, pastor, entrepreneur*

"Veiled Glory" is a must-read for every woman who desires a deeper understanding of God's glorious design of femininity. Elaine Yoder invites us on an exciting journey exploring what it means to be made male and female in the image of God, and as women, to wholeheartedly embrace the beauty and significant purpose of living.

*Sarah Alimowski, wife, mother, women's ministry leader*

It's been over 20 years since Elaine and I worked together in counselor training. Again, she offers a delightful surprise and unveils an engaging portrayal of the image of God revealed, in part, by women. The readers will soon recognize that Elaine serves up a tasteful feast. She draws from her own experiences, Mennonite sensibilities, Jewish rabbis, theologians, counselors and most notably, the Scriptures.

*Merle Herr, husband, father, entrepreneur, counselor, instructor*

Elaine deftly weavers Scripture, commentary, and deeply human stories into a practical and theological narrative. "Femininity uniquely reveals essential elements of the image of God," she writes, respectfully calling us to value the feminine voice in our homes and churches. I am compelled to ponder and seek the quieter, more hidden aspects of God as revealed daily to me by my wife and other godly women. I'm looking forward to using the study questions as excellent conversational starting points among friends.

*Kevin Greiner, husband, father, grandfather,*
*soul care provider, businessman*

# Table of Contents

**Genesis 1:27**

*God created man in His own image,*
*in the image of God He created him;*
*male and female He created them.*

Chapter 1

# Discovering God's Feminine Image

There it was, a gem, lying in a long expanse of sand on the shoreline, its brilliance glistening, nearly hidden from view. The moment the idea was uttered, it sparkled in my heart like a diamond in sunlight. *Femininity reveals a critical part of the image of God.* In a moment, the concept illuminated the reason for my heart's confusion about the significance of women—as reflected in my relationship with men and with God—the uncertainty about me hidden deeply in the trenches of my heart for so many years. The thought seemed too good to be true, yet there it was, truth resonating, tucked into the sand of my heart. A missing gem, this apt metaphor describes not only the dazzle of hope shining into my reality, but also the needed pursuit required to take and hold this precious treasure in both of my hands.

As I move toward the brilliant flash of light, it seems to disappear as quickly as I first sighted it. Another wave comes crashing in; the waters stir the shore. There it is again! My search is back on for this elusive jewel that promises hope and wholeness. If it can be held, it will illuminate the depths of a woman's soul.

The gem is tantalizing, this possibility that the feminine, the core of who I am, somehow reveals essential elements of the image of God while being uniquely female. It so easily slips away, lost in the fray of life. What does it mean if my femaleness reveals something significant, not only about the essence of God, but about how God makes God's self-known to the world? It is a part that is needed to bring completion to the masculine revelation of God's image, not to obliterate or replace it. The feminine can bring wholeness and health not only to me, but also to many, many lives. In a moment, this concept revealed what my heart longed to know, bringing me a deep settled sense of security and peace. Yet it tantalized me. I wanted to know more about how God wants to reveal Himself through me, as a woman.

It is difficult sometimes to know that a woman offers something of significance in a traditional community, especially for a woman who likes to study and explore ideas. The introduction to the image of the feminine *Shekinah glory* written about in the Old Testament, opened an important glimmer of truth to help me understand what I intuitively knew but did not experience.

The first image seen in my mind's eye when I hear "Shekinah glory" is the presence of God in the innermost chamber of the tabernacle, the movable house of God that the Lord instructed Moses to have the Children of Israel build with detailed instructions. The Shekinah glory represents the mysterious presence of God behind the veil, in the tabernacle, and later in the Temple. It required radical respect.

The image of the Shekinah, God's presence in the inner chambers of His house, made me wonder if my beliefs have been misconceptions about what God thinks about women. Those condescending thoughts about being deceptive and weak, thoughts that did not really match the narratives of Scripture. Maybe that is what they were—misconceptions.

What if I *do* bring a significant element of God's image to bear upon my world as a woman? In a world where men lead and are sometimes dominant, it is difficult to know and embrace the possibility that my life symbolizes something of significance about God. I find I am not alone in this struggle.

Not long ago, I was waiting in the seating area of an airport for an early morning departure. In the wee dark hours of the morning, I had driven several hours to the airport to catch the plane and I was happy to relax groggily on a chair, awaiting my flight's departure.

A mother with two sons came into the seating area to await the same flight. Her boys, probably middle school age, were each energetically pulling a piece of luggage. As they sat down, they pulled out electronic tablets to pass the time. Mom sat next to me and struck up conversation. "Where are you traveling?" she inquired. As I responded, she wondered about the reason for my travels. This query coming from a stranger felt pleasant, but unusual. I explained that I was writing a dissertation and was traveling to meet with my advisor. "What are you writing about?" was her next question.

I briefly explained that to satisfy a ministry degree, I was researching and writing about a biblical view of how the feminine reveals the image and glory of God. The level of this woman's conversation and interest led me to explain further. "One of the feminine images of God in Scripture is God as Mother. So, every time you guide and care for these boys of yours, you are revealing something critical about who God is to the world."

"Oh wow!" she exclaimed. "Thank you! You made my day!"

I hope I surprised her with a sense of joy even more than she surprised me by pursuing conversation. The flight was called and there was no more time for further exchange.

Over the past years, as I have researched this topic and talked with many women in various occupations, I have received the same surprised response. From the first pages of Scripture, we find that God created male and female in His image, yet it seems few women know with passion and purpose that they reveal primary aspects of God's image. I have found over many years of counseling with women that this lack of knowledge can have a profound effect on a woman's sense of personhood and value.

I am becoming increasingly convinced that my feminine heart and the image it bears counts and matters in God's economy. I know instinctively that it holds jeweled value. In a twinkling, I have found what my heart has longed to know: that my femininity holds deeply abiding substance respected and affirmed by the Creator of my soul.

## The Treachery of Gender Discussions

I suppose we have all encountered controversy in gender discussions, some friendly and playful, others sharp and barbed. Sibling rivalry may be our first experience with gender competition; at least it was for my brothers and me. Of course, being the oldest daughter dubbed "bossy big sister" by my three younger brothers kept the volley of gender truisms spinning.

"So why did God create a man before He created a woman?" I posed one day at the family dinner table. I quickly offered my reply to avoid any ill-advised responses. "Because one always makes a trial rough-draft before you make your masterpiece," I announced with an air of certainty.

My brother, though, had a quick and witty retort. "No, it's because God didn't want a woman hanging over His shoulder trying to tell Him how to do it," he responded with the same air of certainty. And so, the gender war rages on across the lifespan.

The gender struggle has been around from the first pages of Scripture. The number of these kinds of gender quips is endless and indicates the importance of an ongoing search to understand what the Lord is up to in our gender.

It is amazing how stirring a discussion of the feminine aspects of God's image can be. I have felt it—both the compelling nature of the thought, as well as the uncertainty it stirs. The search to understand the Lord's specific intentions for us as women offers the potential of a deep settled rest in the blessing and goodness of the Lord.

## What this writing is *not* about

There can be so much confusion and easily assumed distortions with any writings about gender issues. It may be helpful to provide some up-front statements to bring clarification to a few of the supporting premises of this writing to avoid potential conflict and uncertainty of intention. First, let's name some things this book is *not* about!

This document is *not* against masculinity but acknowledges that the masculine image offers us significant understanding of who God is to us.

Humankind was made in God's image, both male and female. While this document seeks to discover and name the feminine image of God revealed in Scripture, it in no way seeks to discredit or sideline the masculine image of God—which admittedly, is much easier to see.

God is our Father. This discussion of the feminine images of God does not in any way take away or compete with our understanding of God as Father. Jesus taught us to pray, "Our Father which art in heaven." That is sure, unchangeable, and steadfast. We hold dear to our hearts that we have a heavenly Father who hears and cares for our heart's cries.

We are not as aware of the feminine elements of God that are also present as we call out in prayer to God. The compassionate, nurturing care of God surrounds us as we call out to the Father, for all the gender characteristics are present in Him.

**This work is *not* in support of secular feminist thought or agenda.**

While feminists have used the feminine images of God to support some of their agenda, this work seeks to discover and provide conversation about the feminine images of God that support and promote a biblically traditional understanding of the feminine. Embracing images of both genders as found in the Scriptures helps us to grow in our understanding of the heart of God.

Equally, it is hurtful to men when masculinity is blasted and decried. Masculinity carries a God-given design and call that can be easily maligned in harmful ways. Included in the endnotes is an excellent TED talk presentation you may find helpful which highlights the damage to both genders when either gender is harmfully critiqued or dismissed.[1]

**This writing is *not* against the principle of patriarchy in Scripture.**

The Scripture clearly calls men to lead, with a servant heart like Jesus. As we will see as our study continues, this in no way denies the feminine from a significant place in God's kingdom. It enhances it by revealing the compelling synergy between the genders—found first in God. While the masculine is in the forefront leading, the significance of the feminine brings balance and symmetry to the image of God.

**Why bother to explore and discuss the feminine qualities of God?**

As Christ followers, receiving the image of God in our lives offers healing to our souls as we find our core identity. A new sense of inner freedom allows women to love with abandon as we receive, understand, and embrace the feminine attributes of God. This conversation provides opportunity to mine the gold of God's love and destiny for our hearts.

**The Risks of Failing to see the Feminine Aspects of God's Image**

There are risks in failing to see that God has feminine qualities. This is not being feminist. This is to acknowledge the Scriptural revelation that both genders, as delineated in Genesis 2, carry elements of God's image. Emphasizing that there are only male qualities to God's image omits a very profound and essential understanding of who God is to us in our world. It also omits how both genders are needed to reflect a wholeness to the image of God as God intended it to be revealed.

Embracing the image of God in both genders provides a sort of checks and balances in the relationship between the masculine and the feminine. Each gender brings pieces of the divine intention to relationships. This balance and synergy of the genders, when revealing God's image and intention, is essential for living into our calling as men and women.

In my search, there have been crashing breakers attempting to obliterate this gem of God's feminine images, sometimes carrying it back into the ocean of opposing voices. As I stand gazing at the roiling water, another breaker rolls in. There it is again, that glimmer of light, caught in the brilliance of the sun, beckoning me to pursue its presence and beauty.

In communities where men hold dominating leadership roles, women's voices can be dismissed. John's gospel offers us an example of how Jesus validated and commissioned a woman's voice, affirming the strength and the beauty of what women bring to bear. In John 20, Mary stays at the empty tomb, weeping in her grief, after the puzzled disciples left. Jesus comes to her, revealing His resurrected presence, commissioning her to go tell the greatest message ever heard—"to my brethren." We will look with more depth in a later chapter at this pivotal narrative of Mary Magdalene's encounter with Jesus in the garden tomb.

I have pondered the brief interaction with the woman at the airport so early in the morning. Does she remember the conversation? Does the message of the mother images of God continue to affect how she sees herself, and what she offers to her sons? It takes more than a brief and chance encounter with a stranger to change our view of ourselves without ongoing concentrated focus.

Threaded throughout the Scriptures are feminine images of God, often veiled from view, yet significantly present and powerful, as is the Shekinah in the Holy of Holies. There are many stories of women whose lives radiate the glory of these feminine images, both in Scripture and in our contemporary lives, images worthy of our exploration and consideration.

The Shekinah glory is one image to consider. You may be familiar with some of the mother images of God dispersed through the Scriptures, but did you know the entity known as Lady Wisdom in Proverbs 8 also offers critical images of the feminine aspects of God? There is a sort of "veil" to these images that shroud the glory of God that they bear. I find this fitting and exciting.

It is a worthy search, leading us to find glimpses of the more mysterious and hidden elements of God. Although there is vulnerability in hiddenness, there is also power through intrigue and invitation.

"Veiled glory" offers us a word picture, a working metaphor supporting women living in communities whose practices follow traditional values. These images of God are no less critical or meaningful, even though they are more hidden and behind the scenes. In fact, the power of mystery and intrigue enhances their beauty and desirability.

Many stories in Scripture introduce us to women whom the Lord used to reveal His "veiled glory," powerfully affecting their own and other's lives. These women of old are witnesses to us of the power of God revealed through the feminine heart. A closer look at these stories offers us insight into the essential feminine elements and how they participate in the kingdom of Jesus.

Through recounting the stories of several of the women that Jesus encountered, befriended, and loved, considering their hearts and lives, and the activities that expressed their love for Jesus, we will find a significant guide for living out the images and principles of veiled glory.

Have I whetted your appetite for more? Let us dig into the gold mine that promises treasures for the heart by taking a more in-depth look at these feminine images of God.

## Questions for Personal Reflection and Discussion

1. Ponder and write about your initial response to the concept of the feminine image of God.
    a. What do you feel drawn to?
    b. What resistance do you feel? Why?
2. Do you think considering these concepts in Scripture will be encouraging to your life as a woman who loves Jesus?
    a. Why or why not?
3. What do you think about the concept of the Shekinah glory of God in Hebrew having feminine qualities?
4. At this point in our study, does the thought of "veiled glory" inhibit or enhance your thoughts about femininity?
    a. Why or why not?

**Exodus 25:20, 22a**

*The cherubim shall have their wings spread upward, covering the mercy seat with their wings and facing one another; the faces of the cherubim are to be turned toward the mercy seat…*

*There I will meet with you…*

Chapter 2

# The Shekinah Glory as a Feminine Image of God

Nicole Johnson, a dramatist for the international women's group, Women of Faith, wrote a small book entitled, *The Invisible Woman.* She describes a time in her life when she felt unimportant and unnoticed by those closest to her. One time when she was going somewhere with her young son, someone asked him who was with him. His response, "no one," left Nicole baffled. Why would her son offer that kind of response to the query? Why was she viewed as a "nobody"?

She disclosed the bitterness of that sense of "nobody" to a personal mentor who listened to the questions of her heart. Later, upon the mentor's return from a trip to England, she gifted Nicole with a book detailing cathedrals. Mystified by the gift, the author looked through the elaborate pictures with the description of the centuries of tedious craftsmanship expended on the building of the magnificent cathedrals. Many of the artisans worked their lifetimes without seeing the completion of the cathedral. Some of the craftsman did their work behind walls, using mirrors to visualize their work, hidden away from theirs and other's gaze. The sacrifice of the craftsmen and artisans was stunning.

The question was posed to an artisan as to why one does work that no one is able to view? The artisan's response was simply, "God sees."

A concluding thought from the narrative was expressed in this way. "Maybe that is why cathedrals are not built today. No one is willing to make this kind of sacrifice."

This compelling story introduces an important glimpse into elements of the feminine image of God. While more hidden or veiled, it can be found with focus and search of the Scriptures. We find the feminine Hebrew images of the Shekinah glory, in the Scriptures recounting Israel's journey through the wilderness. A careful look at these Shekinah images promises insight into the feminine elements of God

It has been more than two decades since I first heard

this Hebrew concept of the Shekinah. While the term Shekinah is not a word found in the Scripture, it is widely understood by both Jewish and Christian biblical scholars as the manifestation of God's presence, found most specifically throughout Israel's history.

This idea of the Shekinah and its feminine image was compelling to me. Although the concept lingers hidden, behind the scenes, understanding this primal image offered a promise to me of knowing more about God, while also helping me understand my own design as a woman. The search was on!

In the Pentateuch, descriptions of God's presence with Israel during their trek through the wilderness shows specific images of the Shekinah presence of God traveling with His people. God's very specific instructions were given to Moses for the building of the tabernacle, the movable tent that traveled with Israel. Solomon's temple in Jerusalem was designed elaborately with detailed specificity in a similar design to the tabernacle. Curtains were dividing the outer court, the next inner Holy Place, and finally the innermost Holy of Holies. Hidden mysteriously from view behind the veil, the Shekinah presence filled the Holy of Holies, over the mercy seat, where only the High Priest entered at prescribed times and in prescribed ways.

The Shekinah also carried mother images, nurturing

and nourishing the children of Israel on their journey through the wilderness. As Israel traveled, the Shekinah presence of God went with Israel as the cloud during the day, and a pillar of fire at night.

Maybe you identify with me and Nicole Johnson's opening narrative of uncertain identity. Over the years, there has been a subtle uncertainty about me as a woman, my identity and purpose. Does my life really matter? Am I lovable? Where do I fit? If life is only a meaningless existence from one generation to the next, how could becoming a mother by repeating a meaningless life cycle be fulfilling or an important calling? Would an exploration of the concept of the Shekinah offer me hope in the core of my womanhood? What if I never mother or marry? Does my life hold meaningful significance then?

These sound like teenage questions, yet the residue often lingers, even when life's issues have distracted us from their intensity. "It is time to move on," we tell the (sometimes whimpering) inner part of the soul whispering these questions.

Trips to a local bookstore to pursue an understanding of the Shekinah proved fruitful. As I checked indexes from multiple books in the Jewish section, I consistently found the same definition: the Shekinah was in fact identified as the feminine aspect of the image of God. While Christian theologians mention the concept, the Jewish theological books offer a more comprehensive view.

The word *Shekinah* originates with the writings of the rabbis as they struggled to understand the God that they served. Of course, over the millennia of Jewish history, the concept of the Shekinah has taken on various forms. Many of these writings stand outside of the Christian Scriptures. Amazingly, though, as we look at the accounts of Old Testament writers, words and themes include feminine images, which powerfully reveal God's watchful care of Israel.

While the rabbis reject anthropomorphism, a word that describes assigning human elements to characteristics of God, the Shekinah for the rabbis reveals God's nearness to them. It describes the elements that show God's love and compassion. Their understanding of the Shekinah reveals how God cares for the affliction of the community, even the affliction of the individual. The feminine elements defined in specific scripture passages are specific elements only women can fill.

Some Old Testament passages reveal the Shekinah as mother images of God, the one who labors, gives birth, guides, protects, and feeds Israel with protective, motherly wings. In the next chapters, we will explore these mother images and their powerful implications in more depth.

## The Shekinah Glory in Jewish Literature

Not only is God Father, King, Judge, and Shepherd. God is also revealed through and signified by women, expressed in and through the male-female relationship. The Shekinah takes on images such as "daughter, bride, princess, queen."[2] The final several chapters of Isaiah strongly reflect this concept, where Israel is redeemed and restored to reflect God's presence to the world when God claims her as His bride.[3]

Everett Ferguson, a trusted Christian theologian, begins his exploration of Christianity by acknowledging the importance of Jewish writings to our understanding of the Scriptures. He writes "I consider Judaism the principal context of early Christianity."[4] These historical writings show us how the feminine elements of the Shekinah define and support the traditional view of the feminine.

Shmuel Boteach, a contemporary American rabbi, and Jewish writer, explores the feminine qualities of the Shekinah and the differences of men and women, which "are far from meaningless and arbitrary." He argues for the necessity of the different gender roles so that "women will maintain their mystery." A woman seeks God differently than men, but this should not be "construed as secondary." Boteach asserts that women are more private, and "can find God at home," while "a man does not immediately see God's light," but a man must immerse himself in spiritual pursuit, needing regular public meetings for activities of prayers and pursuit of the Scriptures—"an environment where even he experiences the presence of God."[5] Here Boteach describes how essential the understanding of differences in gender lends to understanding to how each gender experiences God's presence uniquely.

In my years of counseling, I have found what Boteach writes to be true and evident in the stories I hear. The biblical principle of the feminine, through a more private and intuitive way of knowing God, contributes essential elements to the more visible leadership of the masculine. The complement of the genders brings completeness and harmony to the pursuit of experiencing God. Chaos and disruption ensue when gender specific ways of seeing God are not honored.

## The Shekinah Narratives in the Old Testament

Let's take a closer look at the Old Testament narrative in Scripture which provides the primary biblical source for exploring the concept of the Shekinah and the feminine elements it reveals. As we noted earlier, the Shekinah inhabited the Holy of Holies in the portable Tabernacle, and later in Solomon's magnificent temple.

The tabernacle and the temple were the places of

worship designed by God with intricate construction details. Exodus 40:34 and 2 Chronicles 7:1 describes how the Shekinah glory rested in the Holy of Holies, the innermost chamber of the tabernacle and temple, divided from the holy place with a veil. Following prescribed and specific instructions, the high priest entered the Holy of Holies, the place of God's abiding Shekinah presence, only one time a year. The severe consequence of death awaited violators.

The Ark of the Covenant stood in the Holy of Holies. The ark contained Jewish items of remembrance; the engraved stones with the Ten Commandments, Aaron the high priest's rod that budded, and a pot of manna collected during the forty-year trek through the wilderness. Over the Ark of the Covenant was the Mercy Seat, overshadowed by the sculpted wings of the cherubim. It was here, over the Mercy Seat, where the Shekinah dwelt—Jehovah's dwelling place among His people.

The mystery around the Holy of Holies commanded attention and intrigue as the people waited outside for the high priest to offer the yearly sacrifice for the sins of the people. Severe consequences resulted when there were violations of the parameters. God's commands were forthright; "The Kohathites, a group from the priestly Levite tribe, must never enter the sanctuary to look at the sacred objects for even a moment, or they will die."[6]

## Shekinah Images in the New Testament

Hebrews 9 reiterates in the New Testament the Jewish history of how the high priest went into the Holy of Holies only one time a year, bringing the required sacrifice of blood for the sins of the people. An aura of sacredness and mystery surrounded the Shekinah in the Holy of Holies, commanding respect, honor, and a careful reverence.

Some theologians believe the Shekinah images in the Old Testament are mirrored by the Holy Spirit in the New Testament. While that is beyond exploration in this writing, there are significant elements of the Holy Spirit's work and movements that hold elements of the feminine. We sense the Holy Spirit, not loud and bold, but by an intuitive presence that surrounds and nudges one attuned to the Spirit.

## How is the Shekinah discussion relevant to me today?

So, my reader, you may be asking the question, "How is this discussion of the Shekinah important to me today?" That is a good question and worthy of thought. I am not proposing that women should be locked up in the inner sanctum of their home. Never!

A Hebrew instructor informed me that Hebrew nouns do not describe how an object looks, but it describes what the object *does*. We can gather that the feminine Shekinah behind the veil is a mysterious presence. It invites respect. It invites pursuit, but with extraordinarily strong parameters. There is something compelling about the mystery that shrouds the veiled glory of God.

The feminine element of the Shekinah image helps us to understand important aspects of God's hidden, behind-the-scenes nature that is so easily missed. The Shekinah image also gives fabric to God's design of the feminine. As women carry this Shekinah element of intrigue which draws men to desire to know more, so the image reveals the intrigue which increases our desire to know more about God.

Eli the High Priest's sons were haughty and disrespectful men. 1 Samuel 2:12 describes how these sons were "worthless men; they did not know the Lord." They refused to follow the commandments of the laws of worship, operating as priests according to their own whims. Everyone in Israel suffered with the disrespect and violation of the inner sanctuary laws.

Prophetic warnings carried severe consequences for Eli and his sons because of their sin. After these prophetic messages, Israel was defeated by their enemies in war. Eli died when he was informed that his sons had died in the war. The ark of God was taken away from Israel.

The Shekinah, the glory of God's presence, left inner sancuary of the Tabernacle. These were very dark days in Israel's history.[7] "Ichabod" is the term in Scripture that describes the absence of the Shekinah, which means "the glory has departed from Israel."

The Shekinah reveals the sacred value of the hidden, behind-the-scenes elements of God in God's house! This image represents the life-giving element of God's presence in the tabernacle and the temple. The tragedy of Ichabod reflects the empty, lifeless vacuum of the Shekinah's absence.

Pornography, the ogling of the intimate, precious parts of a woman's body, comes to mind as I consider the feminine themes of the inner sanctuary of the Tabernacle and Temple. Porn steals and uses that which is precious and intimately feminine. One who views porn objectifies women by stealing and violating what is most intimate and precious for one's own pleasure.

As we consider feminine themes surrounding the Shekinah glory in the holiest place in the tabernacle/temple, we understand the essential value of women in the home. While the term "stay-at-home mom" can carry a negative vibe in our current cultural climate, the Shekinah image brings rich substance to what a woman's presence brings to her home.

Women bearing the feminine reflection of God bring an essential presence and beauty to their homes. When mom is there, the world is secure and "right." Like Israel, when God's presence and glory is present, blessing abounds. "Ichabod" resulted when God's glory departed, leaving Israel abandoned and empty. Likewise, when the feminine is absent, homes become empty, lifeless, and without light. There is an inner vacuum that erodes a sense of personal security and stability.

Boteach writes, "the highly valued essence in the traditional woman's life is far from meaningless and unimportant".[8] Ichabod shows us the tragedy of marriages when the light leaves "her" eyes, where there is abuse and violence. In the same way, Ichabod images the vacancy that a woman leaves when there is needed marriage separation or after an untimely death,

Women, while more "veiled", are not minimized, but indispensable for light and hope in their family and community. Life-giving creativity and motivation for excellence shapes women as one embraces "veiled glory."

The Shekinah played other significant roles for Israel. The Shekinah also carried mother images, teaming with God as Father, caring for the children of Israel as they wandered through the wilderness. Exploring these images promises deeper insight into God's nurturing care for us and the calling of the feminine heart.

## Questions for Personal Reflection and Discussion

1. Describe how you are impacted by the concept of the Shekinah glory revealing feminine qualities of God.
2. Write out your thoughts about how the Shekinah is more hidden as it reveals feminine images of God.
3. How might hiddenness add power and significance to what the Shekinah brings to bear?
    a. Consider and write about how a more behind-the-scenes hiddenness:
        i. May enhance your femininity in your relationships.
        ii. Lead you to feel more vulnerable.
    b. How have you felt hidden and unimportant in your life? What have you done about it?
4. Ponder and write about modesty.
    a. Do you see any connection between the veiled Shekinah concept and modesty?
    b. How does it enhance relationships?
    c. How might it hinder?

**Matthew 23:37**

*Jerusalem, Jerusalem, who kills the prophets and stone those who are sent to her!*

*How often I wanted to gather your children together, the way a hen gathers her chicks under her wings, and you were unwilling.*

Chapter 3

# God as Mother of Israel

A huge rock formation aptly dubbed "the haystack" dominates one's gaze at the coastline of Cannon Beach, Oregon. With a sort of magnetism, its overshadowing silhouette beckons one to draw near to it. The declaration of the Psalmist comes to mind, "He that dwelleth in the secret place of the most High shall abide under the shadow of the Almighty. I will say of the LORD, He is my refuge and my fortress…"[1]

Haystack's presence and shadow provides a sense of protection from the coastal winds and waves for many little birds and creatures. For some people, it also images the omnipotence and grandeur of our Father God. In His desire to be known by His people, God has written

Himself into Creation with images that reveal glimpses of who He is. Some images, however, are more subtle and easily missed.

I was invited recently to dinner with friends at a young couple's home who had a three-month-old daughter. They served us a simple but delightful meal prepared together by our hosting couple, with intriguing after-dinner fellowship around the table. During our extended conversation at the end of the meal, Katie gently rocked her sleeping infant in her arms, swaddled in a soft white blanket.

I felt stirrings in my heart as I observed this mother gently and patiently rocking her sleeping child. What if this scene of Katie rocking her baby reflected a significant image of God to me? How could embracing this image change the way I view God in the world?

The rock formation at Cannon Beach presents a much more familiar—and masculine—image of God's care and presence. For the many small birds and sea creatures, though, they find cover in the crevices of the rock, where there is a sense of safety and shelter. The image of God as Mother, tenderly rocking her children, sheltering them in her bosom offers a startling, yet compelling image. This is not a bizarre, unknowable idea. It is written in black and white in the Scriptures.

In Deuteronomy 32, the Shekinah is the mother-God who participated in leading Israel through the wilderness. This "mother" gives Israel birth, protects Israel, and guides them like a mother eagle teaching her young to fly. Along with the Father image of God, the mother-God image provides nurturing care: nursing Israel on their journey, feeding them with the richest of fare—milk, meat, and the finest of fruit. Israel grew fat and well developed, like a healthy child with lots of energy.[2]

This passage concludes though, by describing how Israel rejects the Lord by rebelling against His directives even though God faithfully parented Israel through guidance and protection in the wilderness. "You neglected the Rock who begot you, (notice the father image) and forgot the God who gave you birth."[3] I'm told by a Hebrew teacher that the wording of this Scripture describes God as One in the anguish of labor, giving birth to Israel. (Notice the mother images!).

David the Psalmist carries this theme of God as nurturing mother by describing himself like "a weaned child with his mother." The Hebrew term, El Shaddai is interpreted to be the breast of God, the One who nourishes, nurturers, and provides.[4]

Ascribing these images to the feminine is obvious. Birthing, nursing, and mothering are functions that only women are capable of performing.

In the timeless, everlasting love story between God and Israel,[5] the prophet Isaiah uses strong feminine terms to describe God's interactions with Israel. God is described as the one who "formed you [Israel] from the womb,"[6] and then "now like a woman in labor I will groan, I will both gasp and pant." Later we read, "The Lord called me from the womb, from the body of my mother He named me."

The prophet further describes God as mother, "Can a woman forget her nursing child, and have no compassion on the son of her womb? Even these may forget, but I will not forget you."[7] Using one of the most powerful relational images to describe nurture and compassion, the Lord likens "Herself" to a nursing mother where, emotionally and biologically, it is excruciating for a mother to forget her nursing child.

A fascinating article, which wrestles with the mixed metaphors of Isaiah 49, notes the description of God in both genders. The image of a birthing mother "highlights YHWH's constant care and compassionate effort to give the oppressed people a new lease on life."[8] The same Scripture passage portrays God "as a warrior who declares war." The author argues, "that the juxtaposed metaphors of mother and warrior for YHWH in this passage highlights both the compassion and power of YHWH… The metaphor of God as mother emphasizes the feminine elements of God's compassion, while also showing God's masculinity through sovereignty as a king,"[9]

Low's article explores the power of metaphor to help us understand God's revelation of Himself to His people. "The reason we need two metaphors is because there is not one metaphor that will do the job" [of adequately describing who God is to Israel in this passage]. B oth genders are required to present a more complete view of God as our parent. I believe we can safely conclude that it is of the Lord's design that both genders reflect important aspects of His image.

Israel is reminded that they have forgotten the God who birthed and nurtured them. Like a forgotten human mother, God's heart breaks. The feminine Shekinah reveals the mother-heart of God in the shadows or hovering over in the glory cloud, working behind the scenes to nurture, sustain, and protect Israel on her protracted journey through the wilderness. Just as mothers of infants often feel missed and overwhelmed, so God as mother also feels dismissed and ignored by the children of Israel.

I'm reminded of a conversation with a young friend who had recently given birth to her first child. Beautiful pictures on Facebook of this young mother and her babe displayed the joy and beauty of her motherhood. The description she offered me of her labor and delivery added significant details to her story. "I was only a couple minutes from a C-section," she shared. The pain and intensity of the long labor and the uncertainty of the outcome was etched on her face as she spoke. My friend quickly and passionately affirmed my response of "you must feel exhausted when you remember those moments."

This conversation envisions the anguish of the mother-heart of God, who endured labor pains in the wilderness as He does today in His compassion for us. We think of the wilderness experience as being an excruciating struggle and hardship for the children of Israel, but the heart of God struggled in pain with desire and anguish for "Her" struggling children.

Let's talk about gender and pronouns in the Scriptures a bit. It is important to remember that all gender terms ascribed to God are metaphor, images to help us understand something about God with more clarity. Metaphor uses language and images that we understand to bring insight into what is difficult for us to comprehend. While engendered language is used to describe God in both male and female roles, in reality, God is so incomprehensibly more than either gender. It is more than we can ever imagine.

Exploring the feminine images of God not only brings us a deeper and richer understanding of God. It reveals the great compassion and nurture the Lord's heart holds for His children. This emphasis is critical for women, men and for wholesome and harmonious relationships.

A woman's tireless labor to serve her family matters. As with Hagar, God not only sees (El Roi) "the God who sees,"[10] but also is the One who bears our sorrows and meets us in places of abandonment.

In a patriarchal culture where the masculine presence sometimes dominates, the community loses the attributes of God's motherly heart of nurture, compassion, and nourishment. The distortion of God as being only the strong father, the warrior who fights His enemies, or the king who rules with authority, offers an incomplete view of God. When only masculine images are used, God's strength and protection is emphasized without understanding His compassionate nurturing care.

Embracing the mother images of God can positively help to challenge some of the weaknesses of the patriarchal system. A balanced view of the Lord's intentions through gender promises to honor women, mitigating against hideous abuses perpetrated upon women.

## Motherhood and Traditional Femininity

The year that I was thirteen, our family moved to a rural community in a neighboring state during the winter months. It was an experience of paradox and contrasts. I was suddenly immersed in a large junior/senior high school, vastly different from the rural public school I was accustomed to. Conversely, our lives centered around a small church community, rather isolated from the larger world.

It was during this experience that I gained some decided opinions about mothering. The young families at church were large, with many small children.

In retrospect, as I ponder memories from this season of my life, I realize that I sensed the overwhelming feelings of fatigue and despair that enveloped the young mothers. There was constant dysregulated activity. While a nursing baby was crying for attention, toddlers were running around unattended, getting into things.

Witnessing mothers nursing babies was a new experience for me. It appeared indiscreet and contradictory to the emphasis of a woman's modesty in public. I could not remember my mom nursing my brothers. This was all out of my realm of experience.

These young mothers were overwhelmed with the constant demands of crying babies and active toddlers. Their low-grade depression was palpable, a sort of resignation to a demanding life that afforded little enjoyment. At this impressionable stage of life, I could not imagine why a woman would choose this pathway.

Even at thirteen, I sensed a hopeless cycle of existence that would repeat itself again in a few short years. Life had to offer more than this, I concluded.

I feel grief as I look back on that formative impression in my early teenage years. Motherhood looked to me like a dutiful existence relegated to women in a smothering patriarchal world. I didn't have a lot of vision for my life, but I wanted more adventure and purpose than what I saw around me.

Nursing stories like *Cherry Ames, Student Nurse,* looked much more adventuresome and exciting. These books offered dreams for opportunity to explore a bigger world. Being a nurse would possibly spare me from a life of monotonous routine. Being a nurse is not a bad or wrong endeavor, but significant elements were missing from my assessment.

Understanding the mother heart of God is beyond cursory. In the next chapter, we will discover and discuss some profound elements of mothering that recent trauma care research and treatment add to our discussion of what God is up to in describing His image through mothering. These images are critical to us on a deep heart level. As we pursue them, we discover how essential they are to our understanding of the Lord's design of our humanity.

## Questions for Personal Reflection and Discussion

1. Write several paragraphs about what you feel inside when you think of God as Mother.
    a. Do you feel drawn to the concept, or do you want to push it away? Why or why not?
2. The Mother-God fed Her children the finest of fare in the wilderness.
    a. Ponder this concept of God as One who offers good food. Write several paragraphs of your thoughts.
    b. How might this affect how you think of your own food preparations every day?
3. The chapter described a young mother tenderly rocking her sleeping child?
    a. What it is like to think about God's care of the world in this way?
    b. Is it believable?
    c. Have you experienced God's Presence in your life in this way? Journal about the thoughts that surface for you as you ponder this.
4. Spend a few moments in prayer asking the Lord what He wants to show you through your study of this chapter.

# God as Mother of Israel

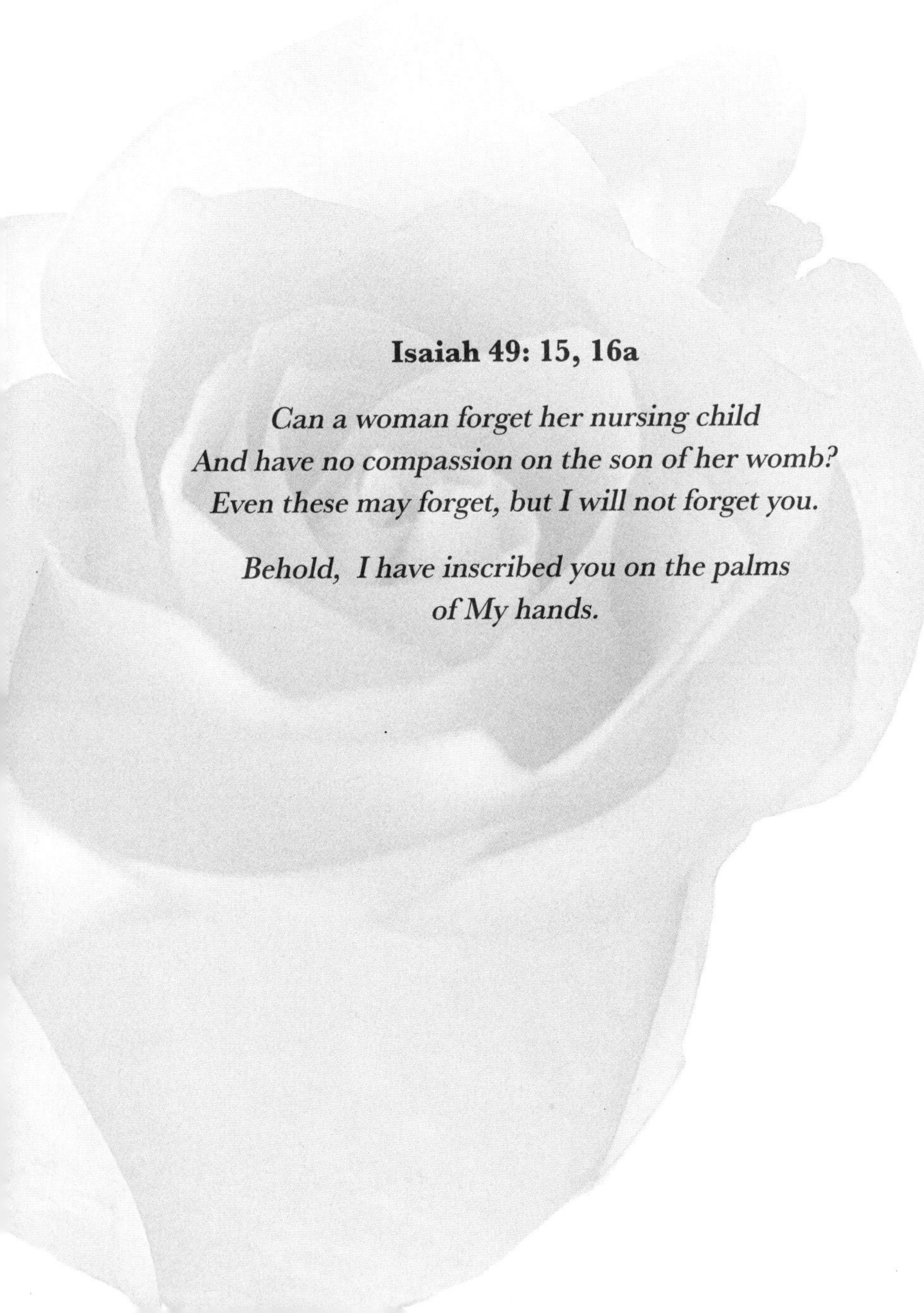

**Isaiah 49: 15, 16a**

*Can a woman forget her nursing child*
*And have no compassion on the son of her womb?*
*Even these may forget, but I will not forget you.*

*Behold, I have inscribed you on the palms*
*of My hands.*

Chapter 4

# Mothering and Attachment

It was during a busy evening in the ER, where I was working as a staff nurse, that a little three-year-old girl was brought in by ambulance after falling about ten feet onto a concrete floor. While she was alert and oriented, there was a large "goose-egg" like swelling in the center of her forehead. Safe practice mandated starting an IV for further rapid treatment in the event of mental status changes.

Starting an IV on a three-year-old is always a bit of a challenge, requiring several staff persons to keep an anxious child still for the procedure. But alas, we were flooded with multiple emergencies and there was no other staff person available to assist.

The child's mother was standing next to the stretcher, bouncing a small infant close to herself while speaking quietly to her daughter. She was calm and steady, and the little girl was peaceful. Just maybe we could manage placing this IV with some careful sweet talk.

After assembling my supplies, I gently explained the procedure of the IV. "I need to put a little 'straw' into your arm for medicine, but it means a stick with a needle. I'll try to be quick, and if you hold really still, I think we can do this quickly." The little girl nodded and smiled; mom added her reassuring agreement. The IV went in smoothly, and my little charmer said to her mother, "Mom, I didn't even cry!"

I'm telling this story, not as a standard of proper child training, but because there was a level of trust and attachment to this mother that allowed this little girl to be brave in a difficult situation. The mother showed a sense of grounding and stability that reassured her daughter of safety in a challenging situation.

Critical elements of relationship between a mother and her child have taken center stage in recent research exploring the impact of trauma on one's personhood. The attachment bond created by the mother with her infant provides the essential building blocks for a secure sense of personhood and identity. Attachment elements established in the first years, even possibly before birth, play a pivotal role in a person becoming a secure and successful adult.

John Bowlby, researcher and theorist, credited as a forerunner in attachment theory, "saw attachment as the secure base from which a child moves out into the world.[1] This secure base developed through the mother/child bond leads to stable, mature adulthood.

Trauma researcher and therapist Bessel Van der Kolk states it in this way:

> "As we enter this world, we scream to announce our presence. Someone immediately engages with us, bathes us, swaddles us, and fills our stomachs, and, best of all, our mother may put us on her belly or breast for delicious skin-to-skin contact. We are profoundly social creatures…[2]

The mother/child bond provides the foundation and platform for a secure sense of identity. We develop a sense of our personhood through the security of the constant, dependable connection with mother who nurtures, nourishes, and notices us, providing for our safety and comfort.

Van der Kolk expands on this concept:

> "Mastering the skill of self-regulation depends to a huge degree on how harmonious our early

> interactions with our caregivers are. Children whose parents are reliable sources of comfort and strength have a lifetime advantage—a kind of buffer against the worst that fate can hand them.[3]

Are you noticing some repeating themes that we've discovered in our discussion of God as mother? The mothering, nurturing presence of God secures our individual identity, providing a safe foundation from which we grow and develop across the spectrum of our years. I believe it is not optional, but an essential part of becoming an alive, motivated, and purposeful human being.

This discovery of the powerful impact of the mother's care and connection with her infant adds significance to our discussion of God as mother. Not only does it offer us insight into the profound importance of what women bring to the world, it shows us critical elements of God's impact upon us as individuals. "The more responsive the adult is to the child, the deeper the attachment and the more likely the child will develop healthy ways of responding to the people around him," Vander Kolk writes."[4] And so it is in God's relationship to us!

Jim Wilder adds fabric to this discussion from a Christian perspective. Identifying himself as a neuro-theologist, (a psychologist also credentialed in theology), Wilder explores the profound implications of attachment, loving God, and character development.[5] This important discussion links directly to the mothering/ attachment themes that we have been exploring. While the Lord can bring healing to anyone's brokenness, the foundational impact of a mother's nurturing love plays a significant role in providing the inner personal sense that establishes personhood, forging the ability of a person to experience the Lord's love throughout one's life.

Trauma research and therapy extrapolate different areas of the brain, how each area functions, and the role these areas of the brain play in the whole of a person's life and relationships. Even a cursory understanding of these brain functions informs effective treatment for inner brokenness related to traumatic experiences. Wilder finds this research significant in understanding the Lord's faithful love and attachment to His beloved children.

Right and left brain are colloquial terms used to describe some of the complexity of brain activity important to our conversation. The "right brain" represents areas of the brain dominated by experiential and emotional data, more intuitive and spontaneous, while the "left brain" operates through an intellectual, processing grid, attune to language and thoughtful interpretation. In healthy brain activity, there is an integration in "right" and "left" areas of the brain functioning together.

Wilder dubs the "right" brain the "fast" brain, acting on data subconsciously and quickly to alert a person to their surroundings. In trauma, the right brain is triggered by the adrenaline rush of fight, flight, or freeze, subconsciously, long before we have a chance to determine danger intellectually. The parasympathetic system works to calm the hyper-stimulated right brain, which in trauma can lead to self-alienation and a loss of a sense of secure attachment.[6] This information has tremendous implications in our discussion of mothering.

Notice how we can link the *fast* right brain, the center of an inner sense of attachment, to how profoundly mothers provide the secure base to the personhood of the children. This secure base attachment provides the foundation for a well-adjusted person throughout their lifetime.

Wilder writes, "A properly trained and uninjured fast track performs many identity functions: individual identity; group identity; social engagement; attachment to our important people; awareness and understanding of other minds; providing moral thoughts and values… maintaining joyful relationships; preserving our shalom/peace… Regulating emotions, feelings, and desires; and more.[7]

"Attachment love (what the Scripture calls 'hesed'…) is the key to access our character… Attachment is the foundation for developing character… We need God's direct communication to the fast track."[7]

Notice how the establishment of a healthy "fast track" in one's personhood connects directly to a secure attachment developed through the nurturing, nourishing heart of a mother. The feminine heart anchors the sense of safety and security in a child's heart to become an effective and mature adult. But it would be easy to miss the most critical component of this discussion.

It is this deep, profound attachment bond, developed through the nurture of the feminine, that establishes an inner security that connects the heart to a secure attachment to the Lord. Embracing this attachment experience in the core of our souls, I believe, provides a critical understanding of the image and heart of God for rich intimacy with His children.

God reveals His image, the deeply critical element of His love, nurture, and intimate attachment through the hearts of women. Our world today needs mothers, women who love and nurture little both ones and all people, with passion and presence to bring essential elements of God's heart to our world. Mothering, however, is not limited to the biological ability to give birth.

### The Single Woman and the Mother Image

It has now been twenty years since my mother had a major stroke that left her entire right side paralyzed. My aging parents rapidly entered a physically dependent season, needing assistance and not being able to navigate life on their own anymore. It was a stage of uncertainty and pain for everyone involved.

I learned so much about life and seasons and personal identity while helping my aging parents. I learned things I didn't know I needed to learn. With new eyes, I saw aspects of the heart of my Father God and the Kingdom of Jesus in unexpected ways.

I learned about mothering, but it was by "mothering my mother," for twelve years after her incapacitating stroke. Initially, the role-reversal was difficult for both of us. Not only did Mom lose her independence, but also the nurturing care of her husband, my dad, when he passed away four years after her stroke.

The difficulties of relationship for Mom and me were sometimes stormy and challenging. Confined to a wheelchair with a growing struggle with dementia, Mom would sometimes angrily say, "I have to go where you push me." I learned, through trial and failure, about the compassionate mother-heart of God, especially when things were difficult. Together we learned, Mom becoming soft and patient, while I became gentler and more compassionate. Offering nurturing care to Mom in this state of need challenged and nourished both of our hearts.

Our opening passage of Isaiah 46 provides insight into the ongoing care and compassion that the "Mother-God" has for "Her" children. Just as a mother's love does not end as her child moves from the stage of infancy, so God's love for "Her" children never ends. With assurance, we count on the nurturing, unyielding, compassionate care of God even as we age.

Single women who have not given biological birth to children also bear the mothering image of God. Compassionate care from the feminine heart is more about a position of the heart than biology.

Mother's Day, though, often represents a day of grief and pain for women who have never given birth. While we celebrate the beauty of motherhood, it can be a day that accentuates the lost opportunity of biological motherhood.

For me, it is a day that highlights the loss of my own mother, of past days, both sweet, with touches of bitter. The sweet memories linger, tinged with the imperfection of relationship, of the goodness of forgiveness and the birthing of intimacy and delight in my relationship with Mom.

Sometimes I receive phone calls and cards wishing me a "Happy Mother's Day." They come from younger people I have journeyed with, whose lives I have nurtured. I feel honored and loved when I receive these messages, yet in the same breath, I feel ambivalent.

I am tremendously blessed by each of the special ones who call me. I also want to bless their relationships with their mothers, however difficult those relationships may be. When my nurture and care help to build meaningful relationships with their mothers, then I believe that what I offer holds significant "mothering."

These phone calls validate for me the mother image of God in my own soul. One important part of all mothering is about building nurturing bridges in all relationships. I'm grateful and honored to be a part of the feminine nurture that our world is starved to experience.

Another feminine image of God, full of delight and mystery, is found in Proverbs 8. Lady Wisdom has much to contribute to our discussion on the feminine elements of God. While offering to us some new insights into the Lord's intention in our gender, Lady Wisdom offers richness and credence to traditional values. We need her spark and intrigue as we push further into the Shekinah images in Scripture. I want to introduce you to this beautiful feminine image in the next several chapters.

## Questions for Personal Reflection and Discussion

1. Write out some of your thoughts about the concept of attachment.
    a. How have you experienced the power of attachment in your life?
    b. What stirs in your heart as you think about your relationship with your mother? In an emotionally safe place, describe your experience with your mother.
        i. What are the disappointments?
        ii. Are there experiences of security and hope? Find a safe friend, mentor, or counselor to talk with about these places of loss.

**Proverbs 8:1-11**

*Does not wisdom call,*
*And understanding lift up her voice?*

*On top of the heights beside the way,*
*Where the paths meet, she takes her stand;*

*Beside the gates, at the opening to the city,*
*At the entrance of the doors, she cries out:*

*"To you, O men, I call,*
*And my voice is to the sons of men.*

*"O naive ones, understand prudence;*
*And, O fools, understand wisdom.*

*"Listen, for I will speak noble things;*
*And the opening of my lips will reveal right things.*

*"For my mouth will utter truth;*
*And wickedness is an abomination to my lips.*

*"All the utterances of my mouth are in righteousness;*
*There is nothing crooked or perverted in them.*

*"They are all straightforward to him who understands,*
*And right to those who find knowledge.*

*"Take my instruction and not silver,*
*And knowledge rather than choicest gold.*

*"For wisdom is better than jewels;*
*And all desirable things cannot compare with her."*

Chapter 5

# Lady Wisdom of Proverbs 8

## Lady Wisdom is Mysterious

I remember quite clearly the day I "met" Lady Wisdom for the first time. It was a bright spring morning. I was sitting on my back patio reading from my regular prescribed Scripture. There she was, Lady Wisdom, dazzling in the sunlight like another jewel to bring fabric and context to my understanding of God. I had already been thinking for a number of years about feminine elements of God's image as this passage provided a stunning new image. I must admit to you, my readers, that this section of our study is the most compelling and instructive to me in my personal journey as a woman. Let's dive in and take a deep look!

Proverbs 8 in many Bible translations is entitled Lady Wisdom. The mystery surrounding this feminine entity described in this poetry has challenged and mystified theologians for centuries. Who is this feminine figure described in subtle terms that eludes concrete explanation?

The proverb introduces us to a feminine entity described throughout the writing as the counterpart of the Creator. Lady Wisdom is difficult to define in solid, black-and-white terms, mysterious, quite like the way women are often labeled. The description of Lady Wisdom offers compelling glimpses of relationship, delight, and playfulness. It seems she brings harmony and goodness to her world. She calls us to explore and search for jewels locked in the intrigue of her treasure chest.

While Solomon is widely considered the writer of this poem, the identity of this feminine wisdom figure continues to be the topic of theological debate. Scholars are fascinated with the rich metaphor found here and have long wrestled with how to interpret the femininity of Lady Wisdom. I have included some details of my research to help us with insight into what the Lord wants us to understand as women.

The Hebrew words describing Lady Wisdom's activities and beginnings are ambiguous and lead to many speculations. Apparently for a few theologians, the feminine descriptions were baffling. In their commentaries, they chose non-gendered pronouns to describe this entity, avoiding any reference to a feminine description of wisdom. A few even changed the gender of the pronouns in their discussion to the masculine! Some describe Lady Wisdom as "the beloved child,"[1] created by God before the creation of the world, or as an Old Testament reference to Jesus Christ.[2] The Torah is another source that some Jewish writers consider, but early Christians would give their own answer to the question of where to find wisdom, as Jesus is portrayed as the word/wisdom "in the beginning."[3] While all of these lend credible thoughts to the discussion of wisdom, let us consider the presence and function of the feminine elements that Lady Wisdom reveals, allowing her to inform our discussion of the feminine aspect of God's image.

"The feminine element of this personification cannot be easily ignored," theologian Michael Fox notes. "First of all, Wisdom is portrayed as a woman, and whatever the degree of the distinctively female in the portrayal, her femaleness is now a fact which the readers cannot escape."[4] He goes on to ponder the feminine presence in this personification and how it brings substance to the Proverb poet's teaching on wisdom. He writes:

"Lady Wisdom is not a king figure. She is

## Lady Wisdom

*Strongest arms and fiercest eyes*
*The song that calms your deepest cries*
*She's quick to climb in, draw in close*
*In children's laughs and wrinkled nose*
*She's in your face, she's mystery*
*She'll kiss your wounds and tie your dreams*
*In her hair gold harmony*
*She'll quiet restless wanderings*
*Life from her very breast, you'll drink*
*Without her hand, confusion bring*
*This haven heart holds purest babe*
*Her voice will shield you from the grave.*
*So wait for her and find her face*
*And love her honor, truest way!*

Sara

> powerful, and she is the principle of dominion, but she does not herself exercise rulership. Instead, others rule by her. Her influence is verbal, working through persuasion and appeal to affection, not through exercise of office and power. Her power and appeal come from the just workings of the universe and the good sense of individual minds rather than from the constraints and compulsions of political institutions."[5]

Fox notes that a male personification in this poetry would change the understanding of wisdom that the poet is offering. "A male personification would make his authority institutional, a derivative of social and political relationships. A male with Lady Wisdom's qualities would be too much like a monarch."[6] This observation leads us to understand that the feminine attributes found in Lady Wisdom add validity and are essential to our understanding of this feminine entity.

Theologian John Phillips concedes that the passage of Proverbs 8 is one of "great majesty and mystery, although one cannot be sure which of the various members of the godhead are [being] described."[7] Interestingly, this author has little problem deciding that the seductress woman of Proverbs 7 and the "Lady Folly" of Proverbs 9 are definitively descriptions of women. Certainly, human women are capable of great manipulation and damage to both themselves and their counterparts. No human woman will, in her own effort, successfully live up to Lady Wisdom's description just as is true for the patriarchal understanding of the masculine. Patriarchy calls men to lead, and yet no human man will flawlessly lead in his own effort to live into the image of God as a king, warrior, or priest.

Proverbs 8 is tucked between Proverbs 7 and Proverbs 9. Phillips describes the downward spiral of a man caught in the trap of the Proverbs 7 seductress.

> "The same subtle serpent who seduced Eve taught this woman her wiles. The downward steps in that first temptation were swift—"[Eve] saw… she took… and did eat… and gave." The serpent kept Eve's gaze riveted on the forbidden fruit so that the look might become a lust… Choice led to a chain reaction… Eve, the sinner became a seducer. The deadly virus was passed on."[8]

Likewise, Philips describes the Foolish Woman of Proverbs 9.

> "A foolish woman is clamorous: she is simple, and knoweth nothing. She may have a pretty face, but she has an empty head. She may have physical appeal, but that is all she has. Any man forced to

live with her would soon become bored with her. Her interests run to clothes and cosmetics, to fashion magazines and gossip columns, to trash and trivia."[9]

While every woman must take to heart the warnings of the foolish and the seductive women, to focus exclusively on these descriptions will miss the author's emphasis on the powerful presence of the feminine counterpart to the Creator. I believe this emphasis provides insight into understanding, with more depth, the feminine image of God.

Lady Wisdom, centerfold in the portrayal of feminine descriptions, shows us the author's point of emphasis. Through a literary device known as chiastic structure, the reader can determine the emphasis of the author's message about the feminine image he is portraying.

David Dorsey, an Old Testament theologian, makes this observation. "In a symmetrical scheme… the center is normally the natural position of prominence," as is [also] true in other places such as symmetrical art.[10] In a chiasm, comparative ideas surround the central point of focus. Dorsey writes, "Chiastic structures frequently have a unique center item… The uniqueness of this location makes it suitable for emphasizing whatever is placed there."[11] Dorsey sees Proverbs 7 through 9 to be a chiastic structure, with Lady Wisdom as the emphasis to the reader.[12]

This chiastic structuring shows us the emphasis the author is making, not only about wisdom, but also about femininity. Lady Wisdom, the co-creating delightful counterpart of the Creator that was formed before the beginning of time, brings her voice. This insight helps us to gather images and motifs that hold the timeless, creative directives of the Creator for the feminine. As women committed to living into God's creative design for the world, we find directives for ways of living into this creative design.

The Seductress and Lady Folly provide contrast to Lady Wisdom. The proverb author cautions the reader against the undesirable characteristics of the feminine that defies wisdom.

Four significant themes in Proverbs 8 bring substance to our discussion of biblical feminine images of God. These four themes are: 1. The Voice of Wisdom and call to "men," 2. Lady Wisdom's impact, 3. her origins, and finally, through a literary motif, 4. the image of wife that Lady Wisdom carries as counterpart to the Creator, bringing life and shalom.

The poem begins by ascertaining Lady Wisdom's voice. She is speaking; she is crying out. This is not from a lectern or a pulpit, but "in the streets, in the market square, in the bustling opening of the city gates, in the midst of urban life… she shouts with joy, she lifts up her voice, she calls, by her spoken word, trying to catch the attention of everyone in town."[13] Lady Wisdom calls out to men, affirming the value of her offerings with a confident voice.

This feminine counterpart of the Creator is present everywhere, not only from high and lofty places of authority, recalling the rabbinic images of the Shekinah as God's presence surrounding Israel. "Lady Wisdom cries out but does not kiss the young man impudently. She desires to persuade with the truthful content of her speech."[14] The basis for this initial aspect of the appeal concerns the truth of her words: they not merely convey mental knowledge, but more profoundly are righteous, straightforward rather than devious and deceptive."[15]

Lady Wisdom knows that she has a message, that it needs to be heard, and that it holds significant value. Her voice, what she brings to bear, is more valuable than material riches; therefore, the pursuit of this truthful and intuitive voice is more valuable than great riches. While this Scripture discloses the significant theme that reveals images of the wisdom of God, enmeshed in the fabric of the text are attributes of an intuitive knowing which bears a quality of wisdom often attributed to the feminine.

In a devotional presentation, a Life Counseling Ministries board member once told us about a time when he learned to appreciate his wife's input into the affairs of their finances. Although he was a man who practiced regularly reading the Proverbs, this experience brought the significance of the feminine voice to him.

This man announced to his wife one day that he planned to buy a number of calves to raise on acreage the couple owned. His wife's response to his announcement was, "I don't think that you should buy those calves."

As a successful businessperson, he felt quite irritated at this response. What does she know about raising calves? Her domain is in the kitchen. His domain is his business ventures. He proceeded to buy the calves.

Over the next successive months, the calves did not fare well. They got sick and needed medical attention. Several of them died. As the project wrapped up, there was no financial gain from the venture.

So how could his wife have known that these animals would do poorly? Did she know? Was this a result of feminine intuition? How much significance does her opinion hold?

Womanly intuition can be discerning, but it is not magic. We all know that a woman does not have unerring discernment. As the story was narrated, our storyteller did not give the reason for his wife's response. He was telling us about a time when he learned the value of seeking and listening to his wife's opinion, even when it did not involve the "kitchen."

The message is not that women always know best, and men must follow whatever a woman offers. What we need to glean from this discussion is how the voices complement and harmonize with each other. *The intermingling of ideas emphasizes that both voices need to be heard to bring completion to the dialogue.*

In the next chapter, we continue to visit with Lady Wisdom. The poetry continues to note the subtle power and goodness that Lady Wisdom brings to her world. She does not rashly confront her world with her wisdom but requires pursuit for her voice to have impact.

## Questions for Personal Reflection and Discussion

1. How would identifying with the qualities of Lady Wisdom change the way you see your personal identity? Explain.

2. Do you find it easier to identify with,

   a. The seductress?

   b. The Foolish Woman?

3. What qualities of Lady Wisdom do you feel most drawn to? Why?

   a. What personal cost would you face as you identify with this quality?

4. Describe a time when your identity has been described as seductive or foolish. How did you find yourself internalizing that message?

   a. Write about how you want to let that poor self-image go.

   b. Why might you find it difficult to let go of the image?

# Lady Wisdom of Proverbs 8

## Proverbs 8:12-21

*"I, wisdom, dwell with prudence,*
*And I find knowledge and discretion.*

*"The fear of the Lord is to hate evil;*
*Pride and arrogance and the evil way*
*And the perverted mouth, I hate.*

*"Counsel is mine and sound wisdom;*
*I am understanding, power is mine.*

*"By me kings reign,*
*And rulers decree justice.*

*"By me princes rule, and nobles,*
*All who judge rightly.*

*"I love those who love me;*
*And those who diligently seek me will find me.*

*"Riches and honor are with me,*
*Enduring wealth and righteousness.*

*"My fruit is better than gold, even pure gold,*
*And my yield better than choicest silver.*

*"I walk in the way of righteousness,*
*In the midst of the paths of justice,*

*To endow those who love me with wealth,*
*That I may fill their treasuries."*

Chapter 6

# The Origins of Lady Wisdom

Lady Wisdom is confident of her role and importance in rulership. Although she is not depicted as a ruler in this passage, her presence and influence are of an essential necessity for the "king" to be successful. Not only wealth and riches are a result of her participation, but righteousness and justice are also a result of her presence and interaction. The reader is left with no question of the role she is claiming to play in the leadership of dignitaries.

"Pride, arrogance, and the evil way" are implied results of refusing the counsel of Lady Wisdom. She acknowledges the power she holds through her understanding, absolute necessities for princes, kings, and judges to lead and "judge rightly."

With this image of the traditional feminine, we find the necessity of both genders, and the harmony that enhances the work that they accomplish together. God's wisdom, in this feminine form, is perfect and true. While neither gender reveals the image of God's perfection, we see the feminine bringing a synergy to the efforts of the masculine to form the beauty and harmony of relationship in God's kingdom.

I'm reminded of a retreat with friends, a group of both married and singles, gathered at a castle for a weekend of fun and fellowship. We were a serious, thinking kind of group that finds grappling with big ideas to be a form of "fun." Activities included teaching sessions offered by one of the professors in the group. Everyone, both men and women, participated in the discussions around the circle. Wonderful times of dialogue, wrestling with issues pertinent to our lives added to the richness of the time together.

Between sessions and group activities, several of the men who shared a significant friendship over the years, congregated in the sitting area of the retreat center, further discussing issues. I noted something uncanny during these informal jam sessions. Several of my single women friends and I, also enjoying thoughtful conversation, began to gather in the perimeter of the little private circle. Although we were obviously straining to hear the conversation, there was never an attempt to include the women to enter the discussion. While the conversation was open to our hearing, the men offered no invitation for us to engage in the conversation.

Although I enjoyed our group times of rich conversation and relationship, there was an undercurrent of uneasiness stirring in me that I could not name. As the group was parting ways at the end of the weekend, I offered my warm goodbye to one of the friends who had not only presented great input but had also participated in the public/private "men's group." To my horror, I burst into tears. It was an awkward moment for both of us, his response being, "I don't know what you want." I didn't either.

It took me a while to recognize that what was stirring was the lack of invitation into the more casual discussions between planned sessions. Let me quickly acknowledge that I do not believe I need to be in the center of all conversations. It was obvious, though, that we as single women were "invited" (or tolerated) to listen from the periphery, but not to be active participants in the discussion.

In our traditional social settings, gender segregation often characterizes our casual gatherings. For some, this makes the gathering more "safe." The idea driving the segregation is to avoid improper behavior between men and women.

Wise and truthful assessment of our heart is always necessary for healthy relationships, but an over-emphasis on gender segregation can create an opposite effect. An unhealthy suspicion about the opposite gender can create unhealthy relationships. More often though, it leads to an avoidance of healthy cross-gender fellowship.

It is significant to note that Lady Wisdom "calls" and brings her voice, but she must be pursued to be found. While one can easily find her in the crossroads of life, she does not exert demand or force to be heard. One must "diligently seek" her to find the wisdom she brings. The masculine, the "other," must seek, must pursue this counterpart of wisdom in order to find her.

As those adhering to traditional orthodoxy, we can grow in discovering new ways for healthy, meaningful, casual conversations between genders. Lady Wisdom provides insight into the goodness and beauty of interaction that brings the voices of both genders to the table.

As one who has participated in settings outside of conservative Anabaptist setting, I have found that my voice is pursued and valued in these settings. A part of the grief that I was experiencing in the goodness of this meaningful retreat with friends from my community was the lack of affirmation for involvement in a more casual setting. I experience my voice and input pursued outside of my community in ways that it is not pursued in my community. Lady Wisdom provides motivation for finding ways to improve healthy discussion and dialogue that brings the voices of both genders to the table.

The strong proclamations that we have heard Lady Wisdom make thus far in our discussion, leads us to ask about her credentials that justify such claims. The poem now moves to the veracity of these claims.

**Proverbs 8:22-31**
**Lady Wisdom as Co-Creator**

*"The Lord possessed me at the beginning of His way,*
*Before His works of old.*

*"From everlasting I was established,*
*From the beginning, from the earliest times of the earth.*

*"When there were no depths I was brought forth,*
*When there were no springs abounding with water.*

*"Before the mountains were settled,*
*Before the hills I was brought forth;*

*While He had not yet made the earth and the fields,*
*Nor the first dust of the world.*

*"When He established the heavens, I was there,*
*When He inscribed a circle on the face of the deep,*

*When He made firm the skies above,*
*When the springs of the deep became fixed,*

*When He set for the sea its boundary*
*So that the water would not transgress His command,*
*When He marked out the foundations of the earth;*

*Then I was beside Him, as a master workman;*
*And I was daily His delight,*
*Rejoicing always before Him,*

*Rejoicing in the world, His earth,*
*And having my delight in the sons of men."*

## Lady Wisdom's Role and Mission

"I was there," "I was beside Him," Lady Wisdom declares of her place at the side of the Creator at the Creation of the world. This feminine entity was "brought forth" before the beginning of time.[1]

Writer Kathleen M. O'Conner makes these deductions of Lady Wisdom:

> "In this poem the Wisdom Woman does not act alone. She is not God, but God's companion... This poem depicts a puzzling mutuality in her relationship with God. She is ever with him, joining in his work, imprinting it with her artistry, and living with God in mutual delight."[2]

This feminine companion or counterpart is there at the Creation, observing all that the Creator is doing.

"It is these origins before the birth of the world which establish the Wisdom Woman's authority. In the ancient world, the older the religious figures and traditions were believed to be, the more claim they had to reveal hidden truths. She is older than even the oldest thing we know, the earth itself. By placing her birth before creation, the author gives her unquestionable authority to speak the truth. This Wisdom Woman is an ancient power to be reckoned with."[3]

Lady Wisdom reveals her origins as being before the creation, before the beginning of time. She was there, observing the Creator doing his work of bringing the earth into being. This claim substantiates her knowledge of how things have come to be and how they work. "Wisdom makes clear that God originated their association. She describes God as the subject who acts and herself as the one acted upon but leaves mysterious exactly *how* God initiated their relationship.[4]

The translation of the Hebrew word, *"amon,"* means, "I was at God's side. It locates her [Lady Wisdom] with respect to God... but leaves her exact role, like her origins, obscure."[5] Numerous suggestions abound. For some, "architect" or "artist," lends credence, while for others "infant" or "darling child" is considered.[6] "Confident and "counselor," is another thought of a writer "based on similar sounding words in languages closely related to Hebrew."[7]

The concept of the "rib" is an image that would appear to lend substantial insight into this discussion. In the discovery of Lady Wisdom's origins, the passage blends elements of creation with gender-sensitive structure. This brings to mind the Creator's fashioning of Eve from Adam's rib, which would show us that God established gender constructs "in His image" before the Biblical creation account. Likewise, according to this

Proverb poetry, the feminine engendered Wisdom came into being. Lady Wisdom "was brought forth," before Yahweh creates the world to be His counterpart and co-creator as He designed the world in which we live. While the text is not clear as to Wisdom's role at creation, what is clearly implied is that the Creator "brought forth" this feminine entity as co-creator before He created the world.

Noting the chiastic arrangement of the poem adds insight into the themes of delight and rejoicing that characterize the last verses of this section. Wisdom was daily His—the Creator's—delight, rejoicing before Him, rejoicing in the world, taking delight in the sons of men. "Wisdom enjoys being with God and her position of honor. Her joy is especially intense as she watches God create."[8]

Theologian Franz Delitzsch sees Lady Wisdom's purpose designed by the Creator as "artistic performances." The description of her is very suitable because, God brought her forth, to join into His creation of the world.

The passage now answers the question of what God had in view for Lady Wisdom's separate existence. "It was she who transferred the creative thoughts originally existing… set in motion by His creative order." He sees Lady Wisdom impacting Creation's effectiveness, artistically… mediating the cause… which the divine creative activity made use of."[9] Ralph Wardlaw states it like this: "Wisdom was the constant companion or associate of all God's plans and all their execution—inseparable from God in all he purposed and in all he did; and "was daily his delight."[10]

He goes on to describe this synergy between the Creator and Lady Wisdom: "As the products of divine power and wisdom successively appeared on each of these days, the almighty and all-wise Creator delighted in the manifestation of his own perfections."[11] Through her important contributions, "Wisdom, by her counsels, when carried into execution, advances the glory of God… there being nothing in the results of her counsels of which she has any reason to be ashamed."[12]

"It is not good for man to be alone,"[13] God says, in the context of the creation story. We see the Creator acting according to His own design and plan. This feminine counterpart brings deep joy and delight to the Creator as they co-labor in Creation.

The power of feminine affirmation rings loudly through this poetry. It resounds of heavenly scenes found in Revelation where the joy of heaven surrounds the throne of God. "New Jerusalem, as a bride adorned for her husband" participates in this scene of everlasting life in the final scenes of Time.[14] This touch of heaven shadows the creation of the world, the synergy and harmony of these divine companions calling to those in God's creation to participate.

Harmonious relationship characterizes the divine interplay of the Creator and Lady Wisdom.[15] This picture of harmony ignites a sense of shalom as this feminine counterpart participates, affirms, and delights in the Creator and His work.

One finds this engendered theme of harmonious delight and celebration threaded through the Scriptures. King David's prayer worships Yahweh as he envisions Israel, His bride, redeemed and taking her place in the temple that David's son would build.[16] King Solomon reenacts this scene of worship at the dedication of the temple.[17] Prophetically, the prophet Isaiah sees Israel as the radiant bride with a gloriously beautiful crown, "married" to her bridegroom,[18] a scene filled with utter delight.

The final act of Scripture repeats this theme of a beautiful bride, prepared, and pursued by her bridegroom, "new Jerusalem, coming down out of heaven from God, made ready as a bride adorned for her husband."[19] These images of engendered, harmonious delight in Scripture form a central theme. Can we support the image of wife for Lady Wisdom from our study of Proverbs 8? The last section of the proverb supports and affirms that image.

**Proverbs 8:32-36**

*"Now therefore, O sons, listen to me,*
*For blessed are they who keep my ways.*

*"Heed instruction and be wise,*
*And do not neglect it.*

*"Blessed is the man who listens to me,*
*Watching daily at my gates,*
*Waiting at my doorposts.*

*"For he who finds me finds life*
*And obtains favor from the Lord.*

*"But he who sins against me injures himself;*
*All those who hate me love death."*

### Lady Wisdom as Wife

The final section of the poem of Proverbs 8 confirms the image of wife for Lady Wisdom's identity as the feminine aspect of Yahweh's image, through the repetition of a poetic motif. "He who finds me finds life and obtains favor from the Lord," immediately draws one's mind to a similarly constructed statement in Proverbs 18. "He who finds 'me,' Lady Wisdom declares, finds life, equating herself to the 'wife' that a good man finds in the later chapter.[20] Donald Treier intertwines the wisdom themes of the chapter with the metaphor of wife.[21] We should not simply listen to Wisdom by studying, but more holistically pursue her via personal relationship; study must therefore be prayerful, pursuing covenant fellowship with God.

The metaphorical—and literal—importance of marriage registers in a parallel between Proverbs 8:35 and 18:22. In the former, finding Wisdom obtains "favor from the Lord"; in the latter, finding a good wife does so. The relational context of pursing Wisdom is frequent and consistent.[22]

The Genesis passage draws one's mind to where the Lord God declares, "It is not good for the man to be alone."[23] Both of these passages affirm the necessary hearing of the feminine voice of discernment and wisdom. In the man's daily life, in his dwelling, this feminine voice brings life. It is not optional, but critical for there to be favor and life for him.

The apostle Peter writes instructions reminiscent of this Biblical mandate. He instructs husbands to "honor their wives" so that their prayers are not hindered.[24]

In the next chapter, we will pull together some of the themes that we've been discovering which depicts this feminine entity, Lady Wisdom. Exploring these themes in the proverb lends insight for women to claim in this co-creator role we have been designed to fill.

## Questions for Personal Reflection and Discussion

1. As you ponder the image of co-creator with the Creator, do you feel side-lined as a woman? Why or why not?
2. Describe the creative marks that you contribute to your world?
    a. How do they make a difference to those close to you?
    b. Do you see them as significant and valuable?
        i. Why or why not?
3. What do you need to experience appreciation for your contributions?
    a. To your family?
    b. To your community?
4. As you ponder these things, what new energy are you finding to maximize your contribution to your world?
    a. Do you sense the Lord's delight?
    b. Why or why not?

*The feminine touch,*
*creating spaces of beauty and grace…*
*enlarging our hearts,*
*inviting us to worship.*

Elaine Yoder

Chapter 7

# Lady Wisdom and the Traditional Feminine

As we ponder the themes of Proverbs 8 and the personification of Lady Wisdom as the counterpart and co-creator alongside the Creator, we discover feminine attributes held by traditional biblical values, inviting us to a richer and more full-bodied understanding of a true, biblical femininity. The seductress of Proverbs 7 and Lady Folly of Proverbs 9 reveal our failure as women, qualities for which we need to seek the Lord's forgiveness and redemption.

Lady Wisdom entices us to life-giving fulfillment of our feminine soul as we follow her example and direction. Women bring the feminine counterpart to the masculine, offering "life" and "favor from the Lord" when she is sought and found. Exploring these themes embedded in Proverbs 8; feminine voice, mystery, creativity, playfulness, and the desire and need for pursuit captures important elements the proverb invites us to explore. These qualities promise to bring enrichment to our relationships and shalom to our world.

## Voice

Having voice, distinctly feminine voice, is a critical characteristic that this proverb assumes as part of this feminine counterpart to the Creator. Although Lady Wisdom does not speak from a lectern or pulpit, she does not weaken or disqualify her message. Rabbi Shmuel Boteach offers a stunning description of the feminine, merging the themes of the Shekinah to bring understanding to the feminine aspect of God's image, and voice in this way:

> "We must not misconstrue woman's more private role within Judaism as secondary. Those who have spiritual fulfillment do not need to shout it from the pulpits of the synagogues any more than those who are truly in love need to demonstrate it in public places. Subtle dignity and quiet spirituality are far more formidable than anything overtly aggressive or physical. True religious piety and holiness do not holler. They speak in a strong and steady voice, resonating from within."[1]

Just wow! That preaches, as I've heard it said in the South. It's so tempting for women to 'holler' to be heard, to raise the volume of our voices when we feel unheard. But it's the strong, steady, kind, and caring voice that invites consideration.

Dana Crowley Jack addresses the importance of feminine voice, and how the loss of one's voice leads to depression in women. Her findings echo the themes from Proverbs 8. "Voice is an indicator of self. Speaking one's feelings and thoughts is part of creating, maintaining, and recreating one's authentic self."[2]

Based on her experience of working with depressed women, Jack names three elements of loss, which affects the feminine soul.

> "First, as the women present it, the loss of self-coincides with a loss of voice in relationship. Second, we notice women lose themselves as they try to fit into an image provided by someone else—husband, parental teachings, the culture… Third, in their narratives, the women indicate that they refrain from speech not only to avoid conflict but because they fear they may be wrong."[3]

The voice of Lady Wisdom is confident of its offerings, declaring, affirming, and blending with the Creator, creating a synergistic harmony. She speaks in a distinct, although mysterious, voice that is steady and courageous, confident of what she brings to bear in her world.

The theme of feminine voice resonates in the counseling office. Often, I hear words like, "I just need someone to hear my perspective." Verbalizing aloud helps one to "hear" oneself, thus assisting one to make wise choices.

Women's voices can become loud and demanding when they do not feel heard. I believe therefore the woman's movement is often off-putting. Increased volume mixed with anger does not improve the quality of one's message or the possibility of being heard. The Scripture warns us in other places to temper our voices to allow the Holy Spirit to be the gatekeeper over our mouths, so that we speak words of life and not destruction. This does not mean, though, to "put up and shut up."

Ultimately, bringing our voice before the Lord opens our heart to re-envision our scope of perspective. The story of Hannah in 1 Samuel 1 shows us a desperate woman, misunderstood by her husband, and scorned by a rivaling wife. Even the Priest Eli misinterprets her as being drunk while observing her passionate cry to the God of Israel.

"No, my lord, I am a woman oppressed in spirit; I have drunk neither wine nor strong drink, but I have poured out my soul before the Lord… I have spoken until now out of my great concern and provocation."[4] We see glimpses of the beauty of Hannah's heart cry.

Hannah's depression lifted. As she left the tabernacle, after pouring out her heart to God and receiving Eli's blessing, she was no longer sad. Naming her desperation with persistence opened her heart to the Lord, changing her.

I believe Proverbs 8 brings to light for women a core sense of one's identity by design. Voice, this foundational element of personal identity, brings security and rest to women as they bring their imprint to their world.

This voice is not controlling or dominate. Confidence allows women to be open to learn from the "other" in relationships. To be like Jesus, we are called to be humble. Awareness of our broken humanity brings carefulness and consideration to the voice of the "other."

**Pursuit**

While the poetic passage of Proverbs 8 begins with the confident voice of Wisdom crying out, the reader is repeatedly instructed that she must be pursued.[5] This feminine counterpart of the Creator, while confident and courageous, requires pursuit to be found. Traditional relationships deem it proper for men to pursue women, especially emphasized in dating relationships and in proposal for marriage. Pursuit is also important in marriage. True masculine servant leadership desires and seeks to hear the feminine voice. Servant-hearted leadership seeks to blend both voices.

This call for pursuit in no way affects the importance of Lady Wisdom's voice of wisdom. Her poise and confidence are not dependent upon pursuit but are required for those who know the need of her relationship. What a challenge sometimes to wait with a quiet heart.

In romantic relationships, we call this being coy. Waiting requires a patience endurance of the heart. It is so easy to minimize one's feminine voice by impatience and demand in any kind of relationship. Waiting bears fruit when a woman finds a way to invite pursuit, and then to wait quietly… before the Lord. Scripture instructs us to ask, seek, and knock, bringing our requests to the Lord.

Like Hannah, a quiet heart knows where to bring the desperation of the heart. While those around us may not understand, we have a "safe place" to bring the cries from the trenches of our hearts. It opens our heart's door to the Lord's inner transforming work.[6]

**Mystery**

A common theme related to Lady Wisdom and to

the traditional feminine is the mystery that surrounds women. A brief Google search yields classic quotes revealing this theme. Grace Kelly is noted as saying, "Emancipation of women has made them lose their mystery."[7] Another contemporary note on women and mystery by Keanu Reeves: "It's always wonderful to get to know women, with the mystery and the joy and the depth. If you can make a woman laugh, you're seeing the most beautiful thing on God's earth."[8] Karl Wilhelm Friedrich Schlegel is quoted as saying, "Mysteries are feminine; they like to veil themselves but still want to be seen and divined."[9]

Shmuel Boteach writes about the mystery of women in his discussion of feminine images of God. "Curiosity and the constant desire to explore the other gender is essential to attraction… the female nature points to a 'feminine mystique' in which a woman becomes ultimately unknowable to a man, thereby guaranteeing the male's eternal pursuit of the female."[10]

Note how commonly held secular beliefs about feminine mystery resonates with the mystery theme of Proverbs 8. The metaphor of "veiled glory," the subtle, mysterious feminine continues to emerge. Notice also how the traditional feminine aligns with the feminine images of God essential, although more *veiled* and behind-the-scenes.

## Creativity

Lady Wisdom participates in the creative work of the Creator. While she delights in what the Creator is doing, she also describes herself as a "master workman," participating in the creation scene.

The Shekinah themes blend with Lady Wisdom, bringing life, light and creative beauty to her world. Utter delight and playfulness characterize the divine partnership between the Creator and Lady Wisdom. The theme of playfulness is not about irresponsibility, but one of harmony, bringing utter delight, joy, and laughter to life.

Dan Allender, a Christian psychologist who does extensive work with abuse victims, describes playfulness as a life-giving category that women bring to relationship. Playfulness offers nurture and kindness which invites healing and health in relationships.

He describes the healing journey of "Katrina." As Katrina's heart healed [from wounds of her heart] and her hope grew, "the larger her soul became for her husband. She tenderly, boldly, wildly, wisely surrounded him with love while allowing him to depart when he got too scared."[11]

This scene wonderfully describes the creativity women bring to relationship as they embrace their feminine hearts. Even in the face of difficulty, as women embrace this playful, creative side of God's image, they bring joy and delight to their world.

Allender further describes the deep sense of shalom that comes from harmony in relationships. "Shalom is a peace that not only recalls all the pieces of one's life but sees how the parts fit together in a unified and glorious whole. Shalom involves rest and gratitude; it provides a momentary balance and harmony where all things seem right."[12]

A fluid dance of relational pleasure provides a vivid picture of the movements between the Creator and Lady Wisdom. I believe the interaction between these entities envision the foundational design intended by the Creator. This creative harmonious dance rests upon the humble attunement to the "other."

Trinitarian relationship and harmony are revealed here. The Father, Son, and Holy Spirit each give precedence to the "other," blending and moving with attunement in harmony with each other.[13] Each member of the Trinity, subservient to the other, creates perfect harmony in relationship. We are invited to join this creative, relational dance in all our relationships, marriage, family, ministry, and friendships.

There is probably nothing that displays feminine

creativity better than the details arranged by a bride for her wedding day. Little girls dream of the day they will walk down the aisle to commit their lives to their beloved. While traditional conservative weddings may not include all the "pomp and circumstance" of more contemporary weddings, the aura of mystery and excitement electrifies the air with expectation.

Israel is the metaphorical bride of God her Maker, her Redeemer. Isaiah announces that God will not give up on Jerusalem, His bride, until everyone sees and recognizes her as a jeweled queen–a bride.[14] Israel had prostituted herself with the other nations and experienced destructive "rape" by her enemies.[15]

God's picture of the redemption of Israel, this prostituted, unfaithful lover that He formed and desired for His own, will one day participate in the wedding of all weddings, when God reveals to the world His faithfulness as a bridegroom.[16] It is no small wonder that gender issues carry such significance in our lives.

Just as the Shekinah reveals feminine images of God, attunement to this image in our femininity opens our heart to God's faithfulness, redeeming and honoring us through our alignment with this glorious design.

Creativity involves far more than one's wedding day. One of my sweet friends, who has suffered deeply in her failed marriage, has learned to listen to the whispers of God's Spirit, finding a special touch when it comes to creating beautiful places, places indulgent in the beauty of nature through the design of her home and garden. These places of beauty provide a place of rich and delightful hospitality. It is in these places of beauty that one's heart is invited to rest, to contemplate God's creation, and moves the heart to sing.

The feminine touch that creates homes of beauty and grace are so reminiscent of Lady Wisdom. Places of beauty enlarge one's heart and invite us to worship. Designing beautiful places takes time, effort, and commitment to create the loveliness of order in our world.

**Modesty and Feminine Hidden Treasure.**

Modesty is a theme that surrounds the concept of "hidden treasure" and the feminine. Our Westernized culture has the capacity to goggle and ogle many things, violating boundaries once considered private. Wendy Shalit has written an important treatise that exposes our cultural disrespect toward the hidden treasure of femininity. She writes,

> "The sexual revolution seems to have failed mostly because it ignored the differences between the sexes—specifically, the importance of female modesty. It failed when women

> began to discover that they were uniquely compromised by a sexual free-for-all, there was an attempt to restore order. Women's liberation may have been a valiant attempt to restore that order, but it, too failed because it was reluctant to consider the importance of natural modesty, and held that all differences we observed were the result of oppression. Hence all their ways to restore order, such as through sexual harassment legislation, have been like trying to put a Band-Aid over an amputated limb."[17]

Editorial writer George F. Will, reviews Shalit's book, pointing out that she has "been accused of prudery ever since she has published a philippic against co-ed bathrooms at her college." He goes on to quote her response, "Modesty is prudery's true opposite, because it admits that one can be moved and issues a specific invitation for one man to try."[18]

Many passages in the epistles of the New Testament Scriptures call women to present themselves modestly.[19] It is interesting to note that as with women in traditional Christian communities, clothing also identifies traditional Jewish women.[20] Clothing choices identify one's allegiance and identity to a community. Through this study of the Shekinah and the feminine image of God, we find that the keeping of a modest approach to one's dress enhances our desirability through the appeal of mystery.

It is hard to miss the connection between modesty and the behind-the-veil Shekinah study we are pursuing. Modesty is not only an issue of the clothing one wears. The apostle Peter validates in women the "hidden person of the heart, with the imperishable quality of a gentle and quiet spirit, which is precious in the sight of God."[21] A courageous, gentle, nurturing heart brings a life-giving presence to those it encounters.

In the following chapters, we will visit with some significant women in the life of Jesus. As we ponder their stories, we discover the heart and acceptance that Jesus held for women, broken women. Their stories give living testimony to the value the Lord places on the significance of our presence as women, though often broken and uncertain. These stories reveal how women participate in the grand revelation of God's redemptive purposes.

## Questions for Personal Reflection and Discussion

1. The chapter material described a synergy between the Creator and Lady Wisdom. Describe the characteristics of the "dance" between them. What would this kind of dance look like in your marriage? In other, close relationships? What new things need to happen for this dance to become more graceful?

2. What is the value in the pursuit of Lady Wisdom? Why might pursuit increase the effectiveness of her voice?

3. Name the ways that Lady Wisdom invites pursuit.

4. If you have struggled with depression in the past, how does the idea of having voice have significance to your depression? Describe ways that you shut down or minimize your voice. Why? Ponder ways you could find to bring your heart's concerns with honor and respect.

5. Ponder and describe ways that you could take your creativity in your home to the next level?

6. Ponder the idea of modesty and feminine hidden treasure. How would your practices of modesty change if you were convinced of the value of hidden treasure?

**Luke 1:30**

*"Do not be afraid, Mary;*
*for you have found favor with God."*

**Luke 7:44a, 47**

*"Do you see this woman?...*
*Her sins, which are many, have been forgiven,*
*for she loved much..."*

Chapter 8

# Learning from Women Who Encountered Jesus

"Greetings, favored one! The Lord is with you… Do not be afraid, Mary; for you have found favor with God."[1] What an amazing message! Hearing that message would feel too good to be true, yet a message each woman as a believer in Jesus would want to hear!

The content of the message that the angel Gabriel brought to Mary, soon to become the mother of Jesus, stands as testimony of someone I want to understand more deeply. "And behold, you will conceive in your womb and bear a son, and you shall name Him Jesus."[2]

Mary's response seems even more amazing. Some of the first words we hear uttered from her mouth are, "be it unto me according to thy word," but only after she inquires of the angel how his incredible message could be true, seeing that she was not married.

We know so little about this woman who plays such a significant role in God the Father's plan of redemption. She gives birth to the incarnate Lord Jesus, God in human flesh.

There is much to learn from this woman who received such an amazing calling from the Lord. There must be clues by which we as believing women can seek that which brings the favor of the Lord.

Mary's humility and surrender must not be overlooked as well as her youthful and favored status. We can understand "That 'virgin' specifies Mary as a young girl of marriageable age (i.e., approximately 12-13 years old) and as a virgin in a narrower, sexual sense... by attention to Jewish marriage regulations."[3]

"Mary's response to the divine announcement... embraces the purposes of God, without regard to its cost to her personally. Her response is exemplary, demonstrating how all Israel ought to respond to God's favor."[4] One can add that this "favored" woman of the Lord offers a powerful traditional example of living into the Lord's favor.

The amazing responsibility that Mary agreed to

take on did not come with the promise of a life of ease. In fact, at the time of Mary's purification ritual at the temple eight days after the baby's birth, a prophecy was given to her. Simeon, "a righteous and devout" man "looking for the consolation of Israel" with "the Holy Spirit… upon him" prophesied that "a sword will pierce even your own soul—to the end that many hearts may be revealed,"[5] mysteriously troubling words that Mary "pondered in her heart."

In our consideration of the metaphor of "veiled glory," the "veil" that we observe in this account of Mary's response to the annunciation is multifaceted. A youthful village girl's status shrouds the role she will play through the centuries of history. Mary's obscurity does not limit, but enhances, the work of God. It is her willingness to believe God's message through the angel and agreement to the use of her body for God's greater purposes that reveals feminine aspects of God's image, as she mothered this special child. This envisions an image of God's sacrifice of offering His Son in bodily form.

### The Woman with the Alabaster Box

Luke tells us about a "woman of the city" that came into Simon the Pharisee's house where Jesus was reclined to eat.[6] It appears to be a gutsy move for a sinful woman with a bad reputation and a negative identity. For this sort of woman to enter the house of a Pharisee is unconscionable. Pharisees were Jewish religious leaders with pristine religious reputations, adhering to the strict Jewish ceremonial laws. Her behavior seems an outright violation of the Pharisaical standard.

One commentator notes, the fact that Jesus was invited to the Pharisee's banquet implies "that the Pharisee has sufficient trust in Jesus' ritual purity to share a meal with him,"[7] yet the woman's presence has introduced a powerful contagion, "a ritual impurity."[8]

What would bring a city woman with this kind of reputation into a Pharisee's house. She was walking into "enemy" territory. She was broken in many ways, the most obvious in the moment was her emotional dysregulation.

Standing behind Jesus, the city woman weeps, so much that her tears make his feet wet, so she wipes his feet with her hair. One senses her attempt to wipe away the shame and confusion of her life, mingled with her uncontrollable flood of emotion. Simon looks onto the scene silently, with scorn, internally noting that Jesus could not possibly be a prophet if he was clueless about what kind of a woman was touching him.

Jesus has a story to tell Simon that compares two moneylenders that cannot pay their dues. The one with the greatest debt canceled will have the most love for the forgiving owner, Simon correctly guesses. Jesus than makes the scathing connection between Simon and the one who "had been forgiven the least." In reality, Simon's huge debt could not be forgiven because his heart was hardened, "he loved little."

This nameless "sinner" from the city, who brings her tears, her shame, and her contrition, receives the glorious forgiveness of the Father, veiled from the sight of the self-righteous Pharisee blinded by his pretentious self-righteousness. The beauty of her broken heart was enhanced by tears flowing from the sorrow of a disreputable life. Jesus had eyes to see the truth of what the world around him deemed as despicable.

"Jesus seeks to bring insight to a Pharisee while responding to the dramatic action of the woman who says no words, but... speaks by her actions."[9] Jesus offered kindness, forgiveness, and the most scathing of all, defense, for this woman, who, in her desperation, dared to enter into "enemy" territory to seek Him. Her courage to stand against the tide of the religious rule of the day to receive the forgiveness and peace for which her heart so desperately longed, offers us an example for today.

The metaphor of "veil" takes on several meanings in this account. Jesus sees the true beauty of this marginalized woman's heart that was not visible to

Simon the Pharisee. The tears and desperation of this woman's heart could easily hide, or one could say "veil" the true beauty of her heart.

We see the theme of the mystery of God embedded in this account as well. While God is not sinful, our view of God is often marginalized by our inability to see the reality of what God sees. This city woman's discernment enabled her to "see" what Simon the Pharisee could not.

The aroma in Simon's house and on Jesus' feet gave witness to the beauty of a woman's desperate heart courageously spilling her gift to honor the presence of Jesus. The same aroma that defiled a Pharisee's house offered a memorial to the One with the greatest capacity to love. I believe, as the city woman left Jesus' presence, her peace-flooded heart had received forgiveness and blessing, freeing her heart to live into her true beauty.

## Questions for Personal Reflection and Discussion

1. Ponder and write about what it would be like to hear the angel Gabriel's message to you.
    a. Could the Lord have a similar message for you? Why or why not?
2. Think and write about the suffering of Mary's heart throughout the life of Jesus.
    a. Was the Lord unfair to Mary? Why or why not?
    b. How does thinking about Mary's life help you in your struggles and difficulties?
3. Describe the desperation of the woman with the alabaster box.
    a. Can you relate to the intensity of her emotions? Tell about a time like that for you.
    b. What did you do when you feel intense pain about some of life's situations?
    c. What would give you the courage to enter Simon's house if Jesus were there?

**John 20:17,18**

*"...Go to My brethren and say to them,*
*'I ascend to My Father and your Father,*
*and My God and your God.'"*

*Mary Magdalene came,*
*announcing to the disciples,*
*"I have seen the Lord,"*
*and that He had said these things to her.*

Chapter 9

# Mary Magdalene, Commissioned to Tell the Greatest News Ever Told

It must have been cool and dark the morning Mary Magdalene and the other women were running to the garden tomb where Jesus' body had been laid. After the crucifixion of Jesus, the women had watched while Joseph of Arimathea had taken the body of Jesus down from the cross, carried it, and laid it in his sepulcher just before the first hour of the Sabbath.

As they walked in those early morning hours, carrying spices to anoint the body, the women pondered how they could roll the large stone away that covered the entrance of the tomb. Arriving at the tomb, the women were amazed to find the stone already rolled away from the door. Shock and horror must have struck their hearts as they viewed the open tomb. The tomb was empty! Running quickly, the women find the disciples to report this finding of the empty tomb.

John's gospel offers many details about how Peter and John ran to the tomb with the women. John, who could run faster, arrived at the empty tomb first, Peter following behind. It was Peter who entered the tomb, carefully noting the grave clothing lying inside the tomb. The face cloth was rolled up, and not lying with the linen wrappings that had been around the body of Jesus.

Gender seems to play a role in the responses of Peter, John, and the women. Perplexed, Peter and John leave the tomb. Maybe there was more danger for the men to be found at the tomb which held such mystery. Why was the tomb empty? What happened to the body of Jesus?

The gospel of John clearly reports that the disciples still did not understand that Jesus would rise from the dead, even though He told them on several occasions that it would happen. They likely were confused. Were they afraid to be found at the empty tomb, fearing they would be accused of stealing the body? Were they afraid of the Roman soldiers?

Despite her fear and tears, Mary stayed in the garden at the tomb. True to the feminine heart, often more emotionally connected, Mary is crying. Grief and sadness seem to overwhelm her. Not only had Jesus died by the cruel death of crucifixion, but now, his body was gone. Mary had been so convinced that Jesus was the Messiah. In an amazing previous encounter, Jesus had delivered her of seven demons. Mary's whole personhood was a transformation to life and health since that deliverance day.

Jesus must have been the most incredible man she had ever met. Her tears flowed in the agony of her grief and confusion. Again, she looked inside the tomb. Amazed, she saw two angels in white sitting at the head and foot of where Jesus' body had lain. The angels asked her, "Woman, why are you weeping?" Before she could answer their questions, she turned around to see a man standing behind her. It was Jesus, but she did not recognize Him.

Jesus asked Mary the same question, "Woman, why are you weeping? Whom are you seeking? It was when Jesus called her name that Mary recognized Him.

There she was, Mary, a woman, overcome by the tears of grief and confusion. I love that Jesus was not offended or hindered by Mary's tears. In fact, it was while Mary was crying that He approached her. Her tears did not change Jesus' mind about Mary's identity or her ability to be a significant player in the revelation of His resurrection. I sense Mary's joy and desperation as she ran to greet Jesus. It appears that she ran to grab him, clutching Him with an energy that said, "don't leave me again! I can't take it. I need You to stay here."

In that moment, Mary did not understand anything but the fact that Jesus was there! The unbelievable was true! Jesus was alive! He was alive again! He truly *was* the Messiah. Now Jesus could set up His kingdom with the powerful message of love and peace. He would bring her people deliverance and freedom from their oppressors. Her sorrow was transformed into great joy!

I am often like Mary in profound moments of revelation. I am amazed at God's presence and intervention in my life. I assume I know what the Lord's up to, and I want to require of the Lord what seems the absolute best for me from my perspective.

It's so encouraging that Mary's inaccurate desire to hold on to Jesus doesn't seem to change His belief in her or the message she was capable of bearing. Jesus gives Mary a firm command to her response. "Stop clinging to Me, for I have not yet ascended to the Father." Mary's demanding energy does not change His further instructions to her. He believes in her voice, in her capacity to present this unbelievable message. Jesus' words are amazing words of affirmation, "Go to My brethren, and say to them, "I ascend to My Father and your Father, and My God and your God."

Jesus commissioned, Mary, a broken woman, to bring the message of His resurrection to His disciples! So many questions loom in one's mind. Why did Jesus not reveal Himself in the garden when Peter and John were there? Why did He wait until after they left to go home? Why did He entrust the message of His resurrection to a woman? Why did He instruct Mary to tell the men?

A New Testament professor under which I studied at a secular university pointed out the gravity of Jesus' appearance and commission to Mary. This revelation of the resurrection by a woman, in a historical way, becomes a proof of its veracity. In the Jewish/Roman culture of that time, a woman's words were not valued or considered credible. No one fabricating this story would ever say that a woman had told it. Through this inverted manner, the fact that Jesus entrusts Mary with the news of His resurrection actually lends credibility to the account.

Jesus makes astounding statements about His Father, and His relationship to Mary and the disciples. Not only was Jesus ascending to His Father, but He also declared that God was Mary's Father and the disciples' Father as well. Jesus was declaring Himself a brother to Mary and the disciples. He was declaring them now to be in the same family. Mary and the disciples belonged to Him, and His Father and Jesus belonged to them.

Jesus' resurrection had reunited the family of God together again! This account in John 20 brings to my mind our study of Lady Wisdom of Proverbs 8. Mary Magdalene becomes a central figure in the revelation of the resurrection of Jesus. She becomes a co-player in the Father's revelation.

Mary's voice first announces the news of Jesus' resurrection. We are not told why Jesus chose to reveal Himself first to Mary. It is interesting to note that Eve, the mother of all living, took the forbidden fruit, ate of it first, and gave it to Adam. One could propose that Jesus' commission of Mary Magdalene to tell the news of the resurrection first, acted to redeem Eve's error. Eve had made a grave error in taking the forbidden fruit and offering it to Adam. Mary Magdalene now carried "the fruit," the message of redemption to the disciples. Through this divinely appointed instruction, the Fall… and Eve's error, were redeemed by Jesus. The resurrection reversed the curse of death from the Fall, offering redemption to all believers.

This account of Mary at the Garden tomb supports our thesis of "veiled glory." Mary's voice, her heart, her desire participated in the Lord's amazing plan of salvation. Mary played an important role in the message of the resurrection.

Mary, and the other women, though often in the background, were valued participants in the Lord's glorious plan for His people. Though more in the background, the women's love and participation at the garden tomb and resurrection were indispensable, just as it had been when they followed the teaching ministry of Jesus.

And so it is for us today as women followers of Jesus. We participate in the ministry of Jesus with loving and nurturing hearts as a part of Lord's family. We can depend on Him, even when we are confused and uncertain, knowing that we can trust Him as the resurrected Lord.

## Questions for Personal Reflection and Discussion

1. What feelings and emotions are you aware of as you go with Mary and the women to the tomb? What experience have you encountered in your past that would stir the same kind of emotions? Ponder and write about them.

2. Based on the account in John 20, discuss what stirs inside of you if you heard Jesus say to you, "Stop clinging to me."

   a. As we can look on in retrospect, was Jesus being unkind? Why or why not?

   b. Have you experienced something similar in your life? Describe.

   c. In your heart, run with Mary to tell the good news to the disciples. What stirs in you as you ponder that?

3. Jesus came to Mary Magdalene while she was weeping. We believe the Scripture teaches that Jesus is the same "yesterday, today, and forever." Ponder and write about what this could mean for you when you are overcome with grief and fear.

4. Spend time pondering what you believe about your voice. Write out your thoughts.

   a. How may this study help you to find courage to

bring your thoughts and concerns to those in your world?

b. How will it change what you believe about your voice?

c. How will it change what you share with others? Why?

## Isaiah 62:3-4a

*You will also be a crown of beauty*
*in the hand of the Lord,*
*And a royal diadem in the hand of your God.*
*It will no longer be said to you, "Forsaken,"*
*Nor to your land will it any longer be said,*
*"Desolate";*
*But you will be called, "My delight is in her."*

# Postscript

The surprising and resounding theme I've discovered over the past several decades as I've pursued this project is this, God wants to be known by us! By creating gender, male and female, in His image, He has "written Himself " into our lives so that we can intimately know Him, and His plan and design for our lives.

As we've discovered in this writing, the metaphor, "veiled glory," portrays elements of the design of the feminine that gives substance and purpose to the lives of women. I believe that through this image, we find shalom in our lives as women. While there are many ways this image becomes expressed by the feminine, through surrender to this creation design we find ourselves aligned with the divine purposes of the Lord's revelation of Himself.

Does the metaphor of "veiled glory" refer to the

practice of women wearing head coverings? For many in traditional communities the answer to the question is a resounding, yes. In alignment with this study, the apostle Paul in I Corinthians 11 instructs women to wear head coverings consistent with the natural order of the world and as a sign of power and authority to the seen and unseen world.

It is equally important to recognize that the metaphor "veiled glory" refers to an inner heart position. Jesus emphasizes the alignment of the heart with one's practice. (Matthew 5:8). I believe it is pleasing to the Lord as we discover ways to align our lives with the Lord's design and intention for women.

I've discovered so much joy, delight, hope, and love in holding the design of feminine close to my heart. I pray that there will be rich blessing for each person that reads and ponders this writing. For both genders, to participate in the magnificent design of the Creator brings an ever-increasing depth of love and beauty to our lives.

# End Notes

**Chapter 1**

1. Cassie Jay, *Meeting the Enemy, A feminist comes to terms with the Men's Right movement*, TEDxMarin, October 18, 2017.

**Chapter 2**

1. Nicole Johnson, *The Invisible Woman: A Special Story for Mothers.* Thomas Nelson, 2015.
2. Barry W. Holtz, *Back to the Sources: Reading the Classic Jewish Texts* (New York:) Summit Books, 1984). 319.
3. Isaiah 62, 63.
4. Everett Ferguson, *Backgrounds of Early Christianity* (Grand Rapids: W.B. MI: W.B. Eerdmans, 2003). xvii.
5. Shmuel Boteach, *Judaism for Everyone: Renewing Your Life through the Vibrant Lessons of Jewish Faith* (New York: Basic Books, 2002), 175.

6. Numbers 4:20.
7. I Samuel 4.

## Chapter 3

1. Psalm 91:1, 2.
2. Deuteronomy 32:13-15.
3. Deuteronomy 32:15b-18.I
4. Psalm 131:2.
5. Isaiah 62: 1-5.
6. Isaiah 44:2.
7. Isaiah 49:15.
8. Maggie Low, "Isaiah 49:14-26 – Who Gave Birth to Zion's Children?" *Trinity Theological Journal 17* (2009), 20-34.
9. Ibid., 27.
10. Genesis 21:17.

## Chapter 4

1. Karl Heinz Brisch, *Treating Attachment Disorders, From Theory to Therapy,* (New York, NY: Gilford Press, 2002), 15.
2. Bessel Van Der Kolk, *The Body Keeps the Score, Brain, Mind, and Body in the Healing of Trauma,* (New York, NY: Penguin Books, 2015), 112.
3. Ibid., 112.
4. Ibid., 113.

5. Jim Wilder, *Renovated, God, Dallas Willard & the Church that Transforms,* (Colorado Springs, NavPress, 2020), 43.
6. Ibid., 43-48.
7. Ibid., 46, 47.

**Chapter 5**

1. Leo G. Perdue, *Proverbs.* (Louisville KY, John Know Press, 2000), 143.
2. Daniel J. Treier, *Proverbs & Ecclesiastes* (Grand Rapids, MI: Brazos 2011), 51.
3. Richard J. Clifford, *Proverbs: A Commentary.* (Louisville: KY, John Knox Press, 1999), 8.
4. Michael V. Fox, *Proverbs 1-9: a New Testament with Introduction and Commentary.* (New York: Doubleday, 2000), 339.
5. Ibid., 340-341.
6. Ibid., 340.
7. Ibid., 197.
8. John Phillips, *Exploring Proverbs, Vol. 1, Proverbs 1:1-19:5.* (Neptune, NJ: Loizeaux, 1995), 171.
9. Ibid., 223.
10. David A. Dorsey, *The Literary Structure of the Old Testament: A Commentary on Genesis-Malachi* (Grand Rapids, MI: Baker Books, 1999), 40.
11. Ibid., as quoted from: H. Van Dyke Parunak, "Oral Typesetting: Some Uses of Biblical

Structure" *Biblica 62* (1981): 153-68.

12. Ibid., 189.
13. Kathleen M. O'Connor, *The Wisdom Literature* (Wilmington: DE: M. Glazier, 1988), 70.
14. Daniel J. Treier, *Proverbs & Ecclesiastes* (Grand Rapids, MI: Brazos 2011), 51
15. Ibid., Proverbs 8:6-9.

**Chapter 6**

1. Proverbs 8:27,30.
2. O'Connor, *The Wisdom Literature,* 66.
3. Ibid, 67.
4. Christine Elizabeth Yoder, *Proverbs.* (Nashville: Abingdon Press, 2009) 94.
5. Ibid, 96. To read several of the multiple discussion of the considerations of the Hebrew word meanings, refer to this author, as well as, Clifford, Richard J. 1999. *Proverbs: A Commentary.* Louisville: Westminster John Knox Press, 99-101; Farmer, Kathleen Anne. 1991. *Who Knows What Is Good?: A Commentary on the Books of Proverbs and Ecclesiastes.* Grand Rapids: Eerdmans 52-56.
6. Farmer, 55.
7. William McKane, 1970. *Proverbs, a New Approach.* Philadelphia: Westminster Press, 357-58.
8. Clifford, 97.

9. Franz Delitzsch and M. G. Easton. 1950. *Biblical Commentary on the Proverbs of Solomon. Vol. I.* (Grand Rapids: Wm. B. Eerdmans, 1950) 191.
10. Ralph Wardlaw, 1981. *Lectures on the Book of Proverbs.* Minneapolis: Klock & Klock, 203.
11. Ibid, 203.
12. Ibid, 204.
13. Genesis 2:18.
14. Revelation 21:3,9.
15. Proverbs 8:30b, 31.
16. II Samuel 7:22-29.
17. I Kings 8:33-43.
18. Isaiah 62:1-5.
19. Revelation 21:2.
20. Proverbs 18:3.
21. Daniel J. Treier, *Proverbs & Ecclesiastes* (Grand Rapids, MI: Brazos 2011), 9.
22. Ibid., 9.
23. Genesis 2:18a.
24. I Peter 3:7.

**Chapter 7**

1. Shmuel Boteach, *Judaism for Everyone: Renewing Your Life through the Vibrant Lessons of Jewish Faith,* (New York: Basic Books), 183.
2. Dana Crowley Jack, *Silencing the Self: Women*

*and Depression* (Cambridge, MA: Harvard University Press, 1991), 32.

3. Ibid., 32,33.
4. I Samuel 1:15,16.
5. Proverbs 8:17, 35.
6. I Samuel 1:10.
7. Brainy Quotes, http://www.brainyquote.com/quotes/g/gracekelly274307.html#BxocC2sAPJ8HBldK.99. (Accessed May 16, 2014).
8. Ibid.
9. Ibid.
10. Boteach, 178.
11. Dan B. Allender, *The Healing Path, How the Hurts of Your Past Can Lead You to a More Abundant Life,* (Colorado Springs, CO: WaterBrook Press, 1999), 45.
12. Ibid., 123.
13. John 14:11-17.
14. Isaiah 62:1-5.
15. Jeremiah 3:6, Isaiah 39:6,7.
16. Isaiah 62:5.
17. Wendy Shalit, *A Return to Modesty: Discovering the Lost Virtue* (New York: Free Press, 1999), 139.
18. George F. Will "Modesty is Sexy. Really. Wendy Shalit, Demure Counterrevolutionary

Urges Women to form a cartel of Virtue." *Newsweek,* February 1, 1999, 74.

19. I Timothy 2:9, I Peter 3:3.
20. Yaacov Yadgar, "Gender, Religion, and Feminism: The Case of Jewish Israeli Traditionalists." *Journal of Scientific Study of Religion 45, no. 3* (September 2006): 354. Accessed October 8, 2012, EBSCOhost.
21. I Peter 3:4.

**Chapter 8**

1. Gertrude von le Fort, *The Eternal Woman,* (Milwaukee, WI: Bruce Publishing, 1962) p. 3, 4.
2. Ibid., 4.
3. Luke 2:34,35.
4. Luke 7:37.
5. Joel B. Green, *The Gospel of Luke,* (Grand Rapids, MI: William B. Eerdmans) 308.
6. Ibid., 308.
7. Ibid., 310.